Treating Women's Fear of Failure: From Worry to Enlightenment

Treating Women's Fear of Failure: From Worry to Enlightenment

Edited by
Esther D. Rothblum and Ellen Cole

Treating Women's Fear of Failure: From Worry to Enlightenment, edited by Esther D. Rothblum and Ellen Cole, was simultaneously issued by The Haworth Press, Inc., under the title *Treating Women's Fear of Failure*, a special issue of *Women & Therapy*, Volume 6, Number 3, Fall 1987, Esther D. Rothblum and Ellen Cole, journal Editors.

Routledge
Taylor & Francis Group
New York   London

Routledge is an imprint of the
Taylor & Francis Group, an informa business

ISBN 0-918393-41-8

Published by

Harrington Park Press, Inc., 12 West 32 Street, New York, NY 10001.
EUROSPAN/Harrington, 3 Henrietta Street, London WC2E 8LU England

Reprinted 2009 by Routledge

Treating Women's Fear of Failure: From Worry to Enlightenment was originally published in 1987 by The Haworth Press, Inc. It has also been published as *Women & Therapy*, Volume 6, Number 3, Fall 1987.

Cover design by Marshall Andrews.

Library of Congress Cataloging-in-Publication Data

Treating women's fear of failure.

Reprint. Originally published as:Treating women's fear of failure. New York:Haworth Press, 1987.
Includes bibliographies.
1. Fear of failure. 2. Self-perception. 3. Women—Mental health. 4. Women—Psychology. 5. Feminist therapy. I. Rothblum, Esther D. II. Cole, Ellen.
RC552.F423T74   1988   616.85'82   87-25132
ISBN 0-918393-41-8

CONTENTS

EDITORIAL

Several weeks ago, I wrote to a woman who had submitted a manuscript to this book, reminding her that the minor revisions I had recommended were overdue. She wrote back, stating that she had taken my letter accepting her manuscript with minor revisions to be a "polite form of rejection" and had not realized that I really wanted her to resubmit it.

Several months ago, I invited a local psychotherapist to lecture to my class on feminist therapy. This woman is regarded as one of our community's foremost feminist therapists. She declined the invitation, stating that she did not feel competent to lecture to a group of students. Later that week, she mentioned my invitation to one of her male colleagues. He said that he would be willing to lecture to the class, even though he admitted knowing little about feminist therapy.

Several years ago, I admitted to a colleague that I felt like an "imposter" at age 27 teaching a class of graduate students. At the end of the semester, several graduate students, all women, told me that they had felt like imposters taking the class and even being enrolled in a doctoral program.

Feminist therapists have all experienced the dilemma of encouraging women clients—often superbly qualified in their fields—to take a risk that might involve rejection or failure. Therapists in private practice have described their clients as "the worried well," indicating that most clients do not seek treatment for serious emotional disorders but rather for transient problems in living. Yet when it comes to women, we should not underestimate just how "worried" or overestimate how "well" clients may be.

This volume contains seven articles relating to women's fear of failure. Based on their research, clinical experience, or personal anecdotes, authors discuss such phenomena as women's sense of their own entitlement, women and worry, fear of success and fear of failure, and women's imposter feelings. Clearly, it is a combination of women's opportunities in society as well as socialization that relates to fear of failure.

In 1973, Jill Ruckelhaus was discussing discrimination against women. She stated: "It occurred to me when I was thirteen and wearing white gloves and Mary Janes and going to dancing school, that no one should have to dance backwards all their lives." It is time that women reach a turning point and believe in themselves.

Esther D. Rothblum
University of Vermont

Women and Entitlement

Brenda Major

This paper is about women's and men's sense of their own deservingness, or personal entitlement. In particular, it considers whether women and men differ in what they feel they deserve to receive from their jobs or relationships, in terms of outcomes such as pay, promotions, power, praise, assistance, and/or services. There is ample evidence that women's and men's performances, attributes, and tasks are valued differently in our society. For example, female performances often are seen as less competent than identical male performances (Deaux, 1976; Nieva & Gutek, 1981), successful performances by women frequently are attributed to external or unstable causes such as luck or temporary effort (Hansen & O'Leary, 1985), and a task or job labeled as "feminine" is often seen as requiring less effort and ability and is seen as worth less than an identical job given a masculine label (McArthur & Obrant, in press; Taynor & Deaux, 1975). As a consequence of this devaluing of women's work by others, do women come to devalue their own work? Do women feel that they deserve less than men?

Everyday observations suggest that they might. Statements such as "I really don't deserve . . ." seem much more characteristic of women's speech than men's. This observation is supported by several recent lines of research which suggest that women have a less well developed sense of their own entitlement

Brenda Major received her PhD in social/personality psychology at Purdue University in 1978. She continues to teach and do research in this area at the University of Buffalo, where she is Associate Professor of Psychology. Her current research interests include the nature, causes and consequences of self-protective strategies, and the social determinants of gender-linked social behaviors.

than men do, especially with regard to certain types of rewards, such as pay for work. This paper briefly reviews the evidence relevant to gender differences in personal entitlement and then examines in more detail why and how such differences might occur.

GENDER DIFFERENCES
IN PERSONAL ENTITLEMENT:
AN OVERVIEW

Reward Allocation Preferences

Psychologists interested in social justice frequently have examined what people feel is a fair or just way to distribute rewards between themselves and others (e.g., Leventhal, 1976). The typical approach used in this research is to ask two people to work on a joint task, give them feedback regarding their relative performances, and then to ask one of them to divide a joint reward between themself and their co-worker. Given this situation, men and women consistently differ in how they allocate the reward (see Kahn & Gaeddert, 1985; Major & Deaux, 1982, for reviews). In particular, men tend to take more of the reward for themselves, and give correspondingly less to the co-worker, than do women with the same performance. This gender difference is especially pronounced when the allocator believes that he or she has performed better than the co-worker. Under these circumstances, women are more likely to split the reward equally with their co-worker, i.e., 50/50, whereas men are more apt to split it equitably, i.e., according to merit or performance level.

Although these patterns may be seen as reflecting women's greater concern for the feelings of others (e.g., Leventhal, 1973; Sampson, 1975), several recent studies suggest that this gender difference is not restricted to situations in which women and men must choose between rewarding themselves or rewarding others. Callahan-Levy and Messe (1979; Experiment 1), for example, examined how women and men allocate rewards to themselves and to others when these decisions are independent, i.e., noncontingent. They found that women and men did not differ in the amount of money they paid to others, male or female. However, women paid themselves less money and reported that less money was fair pay for their own work than men did. Thus, this study suggests that women and men differ primarily in how they reward themselves, not in how they reward others.

Two studies by Major, McFarlin and Gagnon (1984) also support the conclusion that gender differences in allocations reflect differences in women's and men's sense of their *own* entitlement. In our first study, men and women were asked to work individually on a task for a fixed amount of time, and were then asked to pay themselves privately, from a $4.00 pot, what they thought was fair pay for their work. One-fourth of the participants made this self-payment in the absence of any social comparison information; the remaining subjects were exposed to bogus information indicating how much money other participants in the experiment had presumably paid themselves. Results revealed that when no social comparison standards were available, women took only $1.95, whereas men took $3.18. Women in this condition also reported that less money was fair pay for their work than did men. These differences in self-reward occurred even though women felt their performance was just as good as the men thought theirs was. No gender differences in self-pay were observed when there were clear guidelines present as to what others thought was appropriate self-pay.

Our second study (Major et al., 1984; Experiment 2), explored the accompanying hypothesis that if women and men differ in their sense of personal entitlement, then women should also work longer and do more work for a fixed amount of money than men (given that no obvious social comparison standards are present). To test this hypothesis, men and women were asked to work by themselves on a lengthy and rather boring task. Prior to beginning work, all were paid $4.00 and informed that although there was quite a lot of work, our only requirement was that they do as much work as they thought was fair for the amount of money they were paid. Furthermore, they were told that the $4.00 was theirs to keep regardless of how long they worked or how much work they did. As predicted, women worked significantly longer, did more work, completed more correct work, and worked more efficiently than men, both when they thought their work was monitored and when they thought it was unmonitored.

Furthermore, despite the fact that women's work was objectively superior to that of the men, women and men did not differ in how they evaluated their performance.

Satisfaction With Obtained Rewards

Suggestive evidence that women and men differ in their sense of entitlement also emerges from research on job, pay, marital, and life satisfaction. Common observation, as well as theories of social justice (e.g., Adams, 1965; Crosby, 1976), suggest that individuals should feel angry, resentful, and/or dissatisfied when they perceive that they are receiving less than similar others doing similar work. Consequently, one should expect that field research investigating the job and pay satisfaction of working men and women would reveal striking sex differences. Full-time working women in the United States are concentrated in lower paying, lower prestige jobs than men, and women are paid less than similarly qualified men doing comparable work (Treiman & Hartmann, 1981). This difference holds even when men and women are matched on numerous job characteristics that typically covary with sex, such as age, education, organizational tenure, tenure in present position, and occupational prestige (Nieva & Gutek, 1981; Treiman & Hartmann, 1981).

Despite this objectively unjust situation, however, most field studies of job and pay satisfaction find little evidence that women are subjectively more dissatisfied than men with their pay or with their jobs (e.g., Crosby, 1982; Sauser & York, 1978). In one of the more recent investigations of this issue, Crosby (1982) surveyed 345 male and female full-time workers, matched for occupational prestige, on a number of dimensions relevant to satisfaction at work. Consistent with earlier research, she found that the women in her sample were objectively underpaid relative to the men.

Further, she found that although the women were aware of and aggrieved about the underpayment of women *in general,* they reported no evidence of *personal* deprivation or dissatisfaction with their own pay, jobs, or treatment. In other words, although these women realized that other women were being discriminated against, they did not believe that this inequitable situation applied to themselves as well. Thus, women and men paradoxically fail to differ in their satisfaction with their own job-related rewards, despite the objectively documented underpayment of women. Crosby (1982) has referred to this as the "paradox of the contented female worker."

A similar pattern emerges from studies of life and marital satisfaction. Despite prejudice, discrimination, and restricted opportunity, most women report being just as satisfied with their life circumstances as men do (e.g., Campbell, Converse & Rodgers, 1976; Steil, 1983). Studies of family power and task allocations have consistently revealed that wives have less say in important decisions and spend more time on household chores and childcare than their husbands even in marriages where both spouses work full-time (Spence, Deaux & Helmreich, 1985). Nevertheless, studies of marital satisfaction rarely show evidence of greater dissatisfaction among wives than husbands (Crosby, 1982; Kidder, Fagen & Cohn, 1981).

In sum, whether asked to determine a fair exchange with others, or to decide on a fair exchange for themselves alone, women appear to feel entitled to less than do men who have done comparable work. Furthermore, even though women recognize that other women obtain less than they deserve from their jobs, they feel they personally receive what they deserve. These findings are consistent with, but are not explained by, research suggesting that women are less likely than men to engage in a variety of self-enhancing strategies. For example, relative to men, women tend to evaluate their own performances more harshly in the absence of feedback (Lenney, 1977), are less likely to take credit for their successes and more likely to accept responsibility for their failures (Deaux, 1984), and tend to underestimate how well they will perform in the future. How can we account for these differences?

EXPLAINING GENDER DIFFERENCES IN PERSONAL ENTITLEMENT

Psychological theories of social justice such as equity theory (Adams, 1965; Walster, Walster & Berscheid, 1978) and relative deprivation theory (Crosby, 1976) provide a useful framework for attempting to understand gender differences in personal entitlement. A core assumption of these theories is that peoples' *subjective* evaluations of their outcomes or rewards are far more important than the *objective* status of those rewards in determining whether individuals will feel fairly or unfairly treated, satisfied or deprived. In addition, these theories assume that individuals feel deprived or unfairly treated only to the extent that they lack some outcome (or enough of that outcome) and they (1) desire or *value* that outcome, (2) can easily imagine receiving better outcomes under alternative circumstances, i.e., have high *comparison standards* and (3) perceive the *justification* for their existing outcomes as low (relative to·alternative outcomes they might receive) (cf. Mark & Folger, 1984). These three antecedents to a sense of injustice can be seen as corresponding to three different sources of explanation for gender differences in reward allocations and evaluations: gender differences in outcome values, gender differences in comparison standards, and justifications. Furthermore, theories of social justice assume that when outcomes are perceived as unjust or unfair, a variety of cognitive, affective, and behavioral reactions ensue, ranging from psychological justifications of the injustice (e.g., I deserved what I got) to behavioral attempts to redress it. A final explanation for gender differences in entitlement focusses on alternative responses to unjust situations.

Gender Differences in Outcome Values

A popular explanation for observed gender patterns of reward allocations and evaluations is that these patterns reflect underly-·ing differences in what men and women care about or value. This approach reflects the dominant view of psychologists with respect to gender, which is that due either to socialization or biological predisposition, adult women and men develop differing personality characteristics and values. For example, it is frequently argued that women are more communal, status-neutralizing, and interpersonally oriented, whereas men are more agentic, status-assertive, and self-enhancing (e.g., Bakan, 1966; Deaux, 1976; Gilligan, 1982). According to this view, relative to men, women place a high value on interpersonal outcomes such as pleasant relationships and less of a value on self-maximizing outcomes such as money. Women are socialized to be selfless; men to be selfish.

A number of authors have used this type of explanation to account for gender differences in reward allocations between self and others. These authors have noted that women's values correspond to the goals that tend to be fostered by equal allocations, whereas men's values correspond more closely to the goals that tend to be fostered by equitable allocations (Deutsch, 1975; Sampson, 1975). Equal allocations between self and others tend to maximize harmonious social relationships, whereas equitable allocations tend to maximize competitiveness and productivity (Leventhal, 1976). Noting this correspondence post hoc, however, is not the same as demonstrating that sex differences in values or goals underlie sex differences in allocation behavior. The few studies that have attempted to test this explanation directly by comparing the allocations of men and women matched for interpersonal values have proved inconclusive (Major & Adams, 1983; Swap & Rubin, 1983; Watts, Vallacher & Messe, 1982).

Gender differences in values have also been proposed to explain the failure to find gender differences in job, pay and life satisfaction. For example, women are thought to be "contented" with their jobs and pay despite their objectively inequitable treatment because there is little discrepancy between what women want and what women receive from their jobs (e.g., Crosby, 1982; Sauser & York, 1978). This explanation incorporates three major assumptions: first, that women and men value or want different things from their jobs; second, that women and men obtain from their jobs the things they want, and third, that sex differences in job values or wants explain the similarity in women's and men's job satisfaction. In support of the first assumption, a number of studies have found that men report more interest in pay and promotion than women do, whereas women report valuing social relations on the job and "comfortable" working conditions (e.g., good hours, easy transportation, pleasant physical surroundings) more than men (see Nieva & Gutek, 1981, for a review). With regard to the second assumption, there is ample evidence that men receive higher pay and more promotional opportunities than women (Treimann & Hartmann, 1981), and some evidence that women's jobs tend to be higher on comfort factors than men's (Quinn & Shepard, 1974). There is no evidence, however, that women experience higher levels of positive social relationships on the job than men (Nieva & Gutek, 1981). There also is no direct empirical support for the third assumption, that sex differences in job values or wants can account for women's paradoxically high levels of job and pay satisfaction.

A major problem in this area is the frequent failure of researchers to control adequately for sex differences in structural factors, such as access to opportunities, organizational rank, and/or occupational sex-segregation. The American work-force is highly sex-segregated, and most individuals work in jobs dominated by their own sex (Treiman & Hartmann, 1981). Furthermore, pay and promotional opportunities are far greater in "men's jobs" than "women's jobs" (Treiman & Hartmann, 1981). Thus, differences in what women and men may realistically *expect* to obtain from their jobs may shape their values and aspirations (Kanter, 1977; Nieva & Gutek, 1981). Findings of several studies are consistent with this hypothesis (e.g., Crosby, 1982; Crowley, Levitin & Quinn, 1973; Golding, Resnick & Crosby; 1983). Furthermore, the argument that women and men differ in their job values or preferences has been used not only to explain women's and men's job satisfaction but also, as Nieva and Gutek (1981) point out, to *justify* the low rewards that women receive from their jobs relative to men.

In sum, although women and men assuredly differ in their socialization histories, and may consequently differ in the extent to which they care about or value certain outcomes (cf. Eagly, in press), value differences have yet to be established as a mediator of gender differences in reward allocations and evaluations. Furthermore, comparisons of the social behaviors of women and men rarely show the consistent cross-situational sex differences that this type of explanation implies (Deaux & Major, 1986). Thus, the assumption that men and women differ in their values appears as yet to be insufficient to explain differences in women's and men's sense of their own entitlement.

Gender Differences in Comparison Standards

An alternative explanation for observed gender patterns of reward allocations and evaluations focusses on the second antecedent to a sense of deprivation — women's and men's comparison standards. Judgments of entitlement and satisfaction result from comparisons of what one has or could have with some standard. These comparison standards may be based on what one perceives other individuals or groups to have, what one received in the past, what one expects to receive in the future, or even what one can theoretically imagine receiving (Folger, 1984; Crosby, 1976). I have proposed elsewhere (cf. Major, 1987) that as a consequence of differences in the degree to which women and men are valued and monetarily rewarded in society, the comparison standards that women use to evaluate their existing outcomes or to estimate what they deserve are lower than men's. Thus, according to this perspective, the underpaid female worker appears "contented" not because she values money less than men (or values good relationships more), but because she feels she is paid what she deserves: (a) relative to what she expects based on her past pay; (b) relative to what she expects based on what people doing "women's jobs" are typically paid; and/or (c) relative to the people with whom she compares (primarily other underpaid women). Other factors may also suppress women's comparison standards relative to men's. For example, due to restricted employment opportunities or greater home responsibilities, women may imagine fewer and more limited alternatives as realistically attainable.

Consistent with these proposals, Major and Konar (1984) and McFarlin, Major, Frone and Konar (1984) demonstrated that women have lower pay expectations than do men in the same situation. Specifically, they found that female business school students expect to earn less at career-entry and at career peak than do comparably qualified male business students in the same specialty areas. Major and Forcey (1985) also demonstrated that the pay expectations of those doing "women's jobs" are lower than those of individuals doing "men's jobs." In particular, they found that men and women assigned to a job labeled as "femi-

nine" expected to earn less money prior to doing the job and
thought that the pay they subsequently received was more fair
than did individuals assigned to the *identical* job labeled as
"masculine." Thus, simply applying the label of "women's
work" to a job may lower its perceived worth, and perhaps lower
the perceived personal entitlement of persons who do the work.
Recent research by McArthur and Obrant (in press) also has
shown that jobs labeled as feminine are seen as worth less than
jobs labeled as masculine.

Several recent studies suggest that selective social comparison
processes may play a particularly important role in producing
women's and men's differing sense of personal entitlement.
There is ample evidence from both field and experimental research that people are more likely to compare themselves or their
outcomes with ingroup members (i.e., others similar to themselves) than outgroup members, in part because ingroup members are perceived as more similar to the self on relevant attributes, and in part because ingroup members tend to be more
prevalent in the immediate environment and hence more available for comparison purposes (cf. Singer, 1981 for a review). For
. example, Crosby (1982) and Oldham, Nottenburg, Kassner,
Ferris, Fedor and Masters (1982) found that working men and
women are more likely to name same-sex than cross-sex others
and same-job than different-job others when asked with whom
they compare their wages and jobs. Major and Forcey (1985) and
Major and Testa (1986) found that people prefer to compare with
same-sex and same-job others even under controlled conditions
where others of both sexes performing a variety of jobs are
equally accessible for comparison purposes.

By making such ingroup comparisons, members of disadvantaged groups may be insulated against discovering that they are,
in fact, receiving less than they deserve. Ignorance, as the saying
goes, is bliss. For example, Major and Testa (1986) found that a
preference for comparing with ingroup members (same-sex and
same-job others) led to a reduced sense of personal entitlement
and greater satisfaction with a fixed reward when ingroup members were paid less than outgroup members. Of course, this is the
situation that most working women face. Thus, women who are
relatively deprived may remain ignorant of their condition by

selectively comparing with other women who share a similar fate. Furthermore, to the extent that people are chronically exposed to similar others who invest high levels of effort, skill, education, time, etc. in return for relatively low pay or other rewards (as many women are), they may come to see this as a normative standard of deservingness, i.e., a guideline as to what is an "appropriate" exchange. They may then apply these standards in their evaluation of themselves and their deservingness in new and different situations. In this regard, it is interesting to note that Major et al. (1984) found that both male and female participants believed that women would pay themselves less than men, and that women would work longer than men, in their studies. This suggests that shared cultural beliefs exist about women's and men's perceptions of their own entitlement.

Justifications

A third antecedent to feelings of deprivation is the perceived justifiability of the procedures that produced existing outcomes. People who believe that their (relatively) low outcomes are unjustified, i.e., occurred as a result of unfair procedures, should be more distressed than those who believe that their low outcomes are somehow justified. This suggests a third explanation for women's lower sense of personal entitlement and failure to recognize personal deprivation—women may perceive that the procedures that produced their (lower) outcomes are justifiable.

Such perceptions may result from a need to maintain a belief that the world is just (Lerner, 1975), to maintain a sense of personal control over ones' outcomes (Wortman, 1976) or to protect self-esteem (Snyder, Stuckey & Higgins, 1983). The experience of being a victim not only shatters assumptions about the world, but often lowers self-regard. Ironically, there is evidence that people who are treated unjustly but who cannot change their situation may come to believe that they are entitled to less, or that they deserved their fate, rather than believe that they are victims of injustice (Crosby, 1982; Kanter, 1977; Wortman, 1976). There is growing evidence that cognitive illusions (e.g., denial of being a victim of injustice) serve important functions for normal human functioning (Taylor, 1983; Taylor & Brown, 1986). In short, this explanation suggests that for a variety of self-protective reasons, women may internalize their status rather than acknowledge the extent to which they are unjustly treated by society.

Motivational factors, such as desire for control, the need to believe in a just world, or the motive to protect self-esteem, are most likely to be aroused and hence most likely to affect perceptions of justice when ones' *own* outcomes are at stake. This analysis may account for the paradoxical findings that although women underpay themselves, they do not believe other women deserve less, and that although women fail to recognize the unjust nature of their own work situations, they recognize injustice in the work situations of other women. There is less need for self-protective illusions when considering the justice of others' situations. Indeed, Wortman (1976) suggests that it is easier for individuals to see the influence of situational factors (such as unjust procedures) in producing others' misfortunes than in producing ones' own.

ALTERNATIVE RESPONSES TO UNJUST SITUATIONS

As the above discussion makes clear, people may respond to injustices in more than one way. Theories of social justice stress that being unfairly treated is a negative emotional state that individuals are motivated to resolve. This distress may engender a variety of responses which have the goal of eliminating the perceived injustice. Mark and Folger (1984) propose that these responses can be categorized as being directed toward the *system*, the *self*, or toward the *outcome* of which one is deprived. I think they also may be directed toward the *comparison standards* one uses. These responses are not mutually exclusive; an individual may respond simultaneously in more than one way.

System-directed responses. Most research on responses to injustice has considered system-directed responses. For example, a person who feels deprived or unfairly treated may try behaviorally to change the system (e.g., by lobbying for change, striking for better pay, leaving a marriage) and/or may change his or her attitude toward the system, (e.g., feel resentful and angry about a job or spouse). Studies of job and marital satisfaction basically address system-directed responses. When it is difficult for people to change an unfair system or improve their situations, they may be especially motivated to resolve the injustice through psychological means.

Object-directed responses. One way in which individuals may psychologically resolve an unjust situation is to devalue the object or outcome of which they are deprived (e.g., money isn't all that important to me; I really don't want the pressure that comes with promotion) or enhance the value of outcomes that are attainable (e.g., my work is very meaningful; I have great colleagues). Tesser and Campbell (1982) have shown that individuals devalue, or regard as less personally important, those attributes on which they compare unfavorably relative to similar others. A number of other studies (see Taylor & Brown, 1986) also suggest that people construct their personal values in response to performance feedback so as to maintain their self-regard. Note that this argument proposes that women's and men's values are shaped by what society allows them to attain. This causal sequence is the reverse of the argument presented above that men's and women's values shape what they attain.

Self-directed responses. Another way individuals may psychologically restore justice to an unjust situation is to devalue themselves or their contributions (e.g., my work isn't as good; my job is easier) or enhance the value of those who obtain higher outcomes (e.g., his work is better; his job is more demanding). Repeated exposure to outcomes that are unjust or beyond one's personal control may exacerbate tendencies toward self-blame and lead to feelings of helplessness and depression (Abramson, Seligman & Teasdale, 1978).

Comparison-directed responses. People may also correct a perceived injustice by changing their comparative referents. For example, they might choose a different comparison target (e.g., I'm really more similar to Sally than George), choose a different comparison dimension (e.g., he makes more money, but I have a more interesting job), or revise their expectations (I guess my expectations were out of line), so that they feel relatively advantaged rather than disadvantaged. In short, the need to feel better about oneself or one's situation may drive the comparison process (cf. Taylor, 1983).

CONCLUSIONS

The above discussion outlines an interesting dilemma for the therapist. Faced with women clients who underestimate their worth, who are satisfied with far less from their relationships than they should be, or who do not recognize the injustice in their own situations, what should one do? Some might argue that there is no reason to disabuse these clients of their illusions, since raising women's sense of their own entitlement without also making major social changes in the ways in which female attributes, skills, and jobs are valued and rewarded will only foster women's frustration and discontent. Clearly, disabusing women of their self-protective illusions and psychological justifications of injustice will entail psychic costs. For example, a recent study found that those few women who compare their job outcomes exclusively or predominately with men's are least satisfied with their jobs (Zanna, Crosby & Lowenstein, 1984). The far greater prevalence of depression among women than men (e.g., Rothblum, 1982), however, suggests that blaming oneself rather than the system for failing to obtain desired rewards also entails psychic costs.

The alternative viewpoint argues that women will succeed in getting what they deserve only when they recognize the injustice of their own situations. From this perspective, discontent motivates constructive attempts to change a system or a relationship. An example would be the recent efforts of underpaid women workers to promote pay equity (comparable worth). Social change and revolution frequently are preceded by periods of rising expectations and frustration (Crosby, 1982). Elevating expectations may also circumvent a self-limiting cycle in which those who expect fewer outcomes ask for less and in turn receive less than those who expect and ask for more (Major, Vanderslice & McFarlin, 1984). In short, elevating women's sense of their own entitlement may be bought at the price of their discontent.

REFERENCES

Abramson, L. H., Sellgman, M. E. P. & Teasdale, J. D. (1978). Learned helplessness in humans: Critique and reformulation. *Journal of Abnormal Psychology*, *87*, 49-74.

Adams, J. S. (1965). Inequity in social exchange. In L. Berkowitz (ed.), *Advances in experimental social psychology* (Vol. 2, pp. 267-299). New York: Academic Press.

Bakan, D. (1966). *The quality of human existence*. Chicago: Rand McNally.

Callahan-Levy, C. M. & Messe, L. A. (1979). Sex differences in the allocation of pay. *Journal of Personality and Social Psychology*, *37*, 443-446.

Campbell, A., Converse, P. E. & Rodgers, W. L. (1976). *The Quality of American Life*. New York: Russell Sage Foundation.

Crosby, F. (1976). A model of egotistical relative deprivation. *Psychological Review*, *83*, 85-113.

Crosby, F. (1982). *Relative deprivation and working women*. New York: Oxford University Press.

Crowley, J., Levitin, T. E. & Quinn, R. P. (1973). Seven deadly half-truths about women. In C. Tavris (ed.), *The female experience*. Del Map, CA: CRM.

Deaux, K. (1976). *The behavior of women and men*. Monterey, CA: Brooks/Cole.

Deaux, K. (1984). From individual differences to social categories: Analysis of a decade's research on gender. *American Psychologist*, *39*, 105-116.

Deaux, K. & Major, B. (1986). Putting gender into context: An interactive model of gender-related behavior. Manuscript under review. SUNY at Buffalo, Buffalo, NY

Deutsch, M. (1975). Equity, equality and need: What determines which value will be used as the basis of distributive justice? *Journal of Social Issues*, *31*, 137-149.

Eagly, A. H. (in press). *Sex differences in social behavior: A social-role interpretation*. Erlbaum.

Folger, R. (1984, July). Rethinking equity theory: A referent cognitions model. Paper presented at the NSF Cross-National Conference on Justice in Intergroup Relations, Morburg, West Germany.

Golding, J., Resnick, A. & Crosby, F. (1983). Work satisfaction as a function of gender and job status. *Psychology of Women Quarterly*, *1*, 286-290.

Gilligan, C. (1982). *In a different voice*. Cambridge, MA: Harvard University Press.

Hansen, R. D. & O'Leary, V. E. (1985). Sex-determined attributions. In V. E. O'Leary, R. K. Unger & B. S. Wallston (eds.), *Women, gender, and social psychology*. (pp. 67-100). Hillsdale, NJ: Lawrence Erlbaum.

Kahn, A. S. & Gaeddert, W. P. (1985). From theories of equity to theories of justice: The liberating consequences of studying women. In V. E. O'Leary, R. K. Unger & B. S. Wallston (eds.), *Women, gender, and social psychology*. (pp. 129-148). Hillsdale, NJ: Lawrence Erlbaum.

Kanter, R. M. (1977). *Men and women of the corporation*. New York: Basic Books.

Lenny, E. (1977). Women's self-confidence in achievement settings. *Psychology Bulletin*, *84*, 1-13.

Lerner, M. J. (1975). The justice motive in social behavior: An introduction, *Journal of Social Issues*, *31*, 1-19.

Leventhal, G. S. (1976). The distribution of rewards and resources in groups and organizations. In L. Berkowitz and E. Walster (eds.), *Advances in experimental social psychology*, (Vol. 9 pp. 92-133). New York: Academic Press.

MacArthur, L. Z. & Obrant, S. W. (in press). Sex biases in comparable worth analyses. *Journal of Applied Social Psychology*.

Major, B. & Adams, J. B. (1983). The role of gender, interpersonal orientation and self-presentation is distributive justice behavior. *Journal of Personality and Social Psychology, 45,* 598-608.

Major, B. & Adams, J. B. (1984). Situational moderators of gender differences in reward allocations. *Sex roles, 11,* 869-880.

Major, B. & Deaux, K. (1982). Individual differences in justice behavior. In J. Greenberg and R. L. Cohen (eds.), *Equity and justice in social behavior.* (pp. 43-76). New York: Academic Press.

Major, B. & Forcey, B. (1985). Social comparisons and pay evaluations: Preferences for same-sex and same-job wage comparisons. *Journal of Experimental Social Psychology, 21,* 393-405.

Major, B. & Konar, E. (1984). An investigation of sex differences in pay expectations and their possible causes. *Academy of Management Journal, 27,* 777-792.

Major, B., McFarlin, D. & Gagnon, D. (1984). Overworked and underpaid: On the nature of gender differences in personal entitlement. *Journal of Personality and Social Psychology, 47,* 1399-1412.

Major, B. & Testa, M. (1986). The role of social comparison processes in judgments of entitlement and satisfaction. Manuscript under review. State University of New York at Buffalo, Psychology Department, Buffalo, NY

Major, B., Vanderslice, V. & McFarlin, D. B. (1984). Effects of pay expected on pay received: The confirmatory nature of initial expectations. *Journal of Applied Psychology, 14,* 399-412.

Major, B. (1987). Gender, justice, and the psychology of entitlement. In P. Shaver and C. Hendrick (eds.), *Review of personality and social psychology.* (Vol. 7) Newbury Park, CA: Sage.

Mark, M. A. & Folger, F. (1984). Responses to relative deprivation: A conceptual framework. In P. Shaver (ed.), *Review of Personality and Social Psychology.* (Vol. 5, pp. 192-218). Beverly Hills, CA: Sage.

McFarlin, D. B., Major, B., Frone, M. & Konar, E. (1984, August). Predicting management students' pay expectations: The importance of social comparisons. Paper presented at the meeting of the American Psychological Association, Toronto, Canada.

Nieva, V. F. & Gutek, B. A. (1981). *Women and work: A psychological perspective.* New York, NY: Praeger.

Oldham, G. R., Nottenburg, G., Kassner, M. W., Ferris, G., Fedor, D. & Masters, M. (1982). The selection and consequences of job comparisons. *Organizational Behavior and Human Performance, 29,* 84-111.

Quinn, R. L. & Shepard, L. (1974). *The 1972-73 quality of employment survey.* Ann Arbor, MI: Survey Research Center.

Rothblum, E. (1982). Women's socialization and the prevalence of depression: The feminine mistake. *Women & Therapy,* 5-13.

Sampson, E. E. (1975). Justice as equality. *Journal of Social Issues, 31,* 45-61.

Sauser, W. I. & York, M. (1978). Sex differences in job satisfaction: A reexamination. *Personnel Psychology, 31,* 537-547.

Singer, E. (1981). Reference groups and social evaluations. In M. Rosenberg & R. H. Turner (eds.), *Social psychology: Sociological perspectives.* (pp. 66-93). New York: Basic Books.

Snyder, C. R., Higgins, R. L. & Stucky, R. J. (1983). Excuses: Masquerades in search of grace. New York: John Wiley & Sons.

Swap, W. & Rubin, J. Z. (1983). Measurement of interpersonal orientation. *Journal of Personality and Social Psychology, 44,* 208-219.

Taylor, S. E. (1983). Adjustment to threatening events: A theory of cognitive adaptation. *American Psychologist*, 1161-1173.

Taylor, S. E. & Brown (1986). Social psychological contributions to a theory of mental health. Manuscript submitted for publication.

Tesser, A. & Campbell, J. (1982). Self-definition and self-evaluation maintenance. In J. Sulls & A. Greenwald (eds.), *Psychological Perspectives on the self.* (pp. 1-31). Hillsdale, NJ: Lawrence Erlbaum.

Treiman, D. J. & Hartmann, H. I. (1981). *Women, work and wages: Equal pay for jobs of equal value.* Washington, DC: National Academy Press.

Walster, E., Walster, G. W. & Berscheid, E. (1978). *Equity: Theory and research.* Boston: Allyn & Bacon.

Watts, B. L., Vallacher, R. R. & Messe, L. A. (1982). Toward understanding sex differences in pay allocations: Agency communion, and reward distribution behavior. *Sex Roles, 12,* 1175-1188.

Wortman, C. B. (1976). Causal attributions and personal control. In J. H. Harvey, W. J. Ickes & R. F. Kidd (eds.), *New Directions in Attribution Research*, (Vol. 1, pp. 23-52). Hillsdale, NJ: Lawrence Erlbaum.

Zanna, M. P., Crosby, F. & Loewenstein, G. (1984). Male reference groups and job satisfaction among female professionals. Presented at meeting of American Psychological Association, Toronto, Canada.

Fear of Failure in Women

Lenora M. Yuen
Devora S. Depper

A 45 year-old professional woman says tearfully that nothing she does is ever "good enough," in spite of the fact that she has been awarded numerous promotions and awards. A very bright college student describes her long-standing pattern of procrastination on academic work, starting off at the top of the class at the outset of each semester and ending up with a grade of "incomplete." A 32 year-old single woman nonchalantly states that she expects to be single her entire life since an intimate relationship demands sacrificing her independence.

These women, and many others like them, show up in the therapists' offices all around the country. Over and over again, they relate stories which touch on familiar themes: the longing for respect and recognition, the desire for acceptance, and the wish to be loved. What makes these themes so powerful and poignant is the belief, stated explicitly or only implied, that such longings are doomed never to be satisfied. No matter what she does, how hard she works, or how "good" she tries to be, such a woman fears that she will never be "good enough." She fears that she will be a failure, if not in others' eyes then certainly in her own.

Lenora M. Yuen is a clinical psychologist in private practice, 667 Lytton Avenue, Palo Alto, CA 94301.

Devora S. Depper is Assistant Clinical Professor of Psychology, Langley Porter Psychiatric Institute, University of California, San Francisco, and a clinical psychologist in private practice, 457 Spruce Street, San Francisco, CA 94118.

The authors would like to express their appreciation to Barbara Kaplan, PhD, and John Peters, PhD, who offered editorial suggestions on this manuscript.

Requests for reprints may be addressed to either author.

21

There are several strategies for coping with fear of failure. A woman may underachieve by retreating from competition, not making a full-out effort, avoiding new challenges, procrastinating until the very last minute, or maintaining a disinterested or apathetic attitude. A woman may, on the other hand, overachieve by taking on too much responsibility, trying to be a "superwoman," or being overly conscientious and compliant. Either way, the toll can be significant. A woman who lives with the fear of failure can never rest; she can never fully be herself or be at peace with herself because she holds herself to a standard that demands no less than perfection. When a woman fears failure, there is always a stone still unturned or a mountain to be scaled. At any moment, someone could discover her inadequacy. All too often, this is the woman who tries to do everything, but is able to enjoy nothing.

In this article we would like to explore fear of failure in women: what it is and how it is manifest, how it has been viewed in the literature, and how we can understand it in light of changing conceptualizations of women's development. We are not going to address the complexities of these phenomena for men. Neither will we differentiate between what may be women's issues and issues that are universal for both sexes. And, while we will discuss some of the literature, this is not meant to be an exhaustive review. Although fear of failure is often seen as a ubiquitous artifact of the ever-increasing pressures in contemporary society, it is our contention that fear of failure in women must be examined not only within the context of broad social and developmental norms, but also within the context of the intrapsychic dynamics of any individual's own life story. Our model for understanding fear of failure in women is an attempt to integrate both the socio-psychological and the intrapsychic dimensions of female psychology.

WHAT IS FEAR OF FAILURE?

A Definition

In our view, fear of failure is an internal experience related to achievement. It is not necessarily related to external, objective measures of success or failure, such as promotion or job loss, a passing or failing grade, or rave reviews of the dinner party last Saturday. A person can fail in actuality and not have any inner conflict or anxiety about having failed. Conversely, a person may succeed by all objective or conventional standards and still have an internal experience of having failed. Thus, a woman may get an A on a test, but if she thinks that she should have gotten the highest score in the class and came in second, she may experience herself as having failed.

"Failure" is the experience of falling short, whether or not one actually does so. It is the discrepancy between a self-set expectation or standard, and the self-perceived accomplishment. In this regard, we are in basic agreement with writers such as Birney, Burdick and Teevan (1969), Beery (1975), and Burka and Yuen (1983), all of whom emphasize that people who fear failure avoid the internal *experience* of failure, not objective failure itself. Indeed, one may bring on objective failure precisely in order not to feel internally that one has failed.

The question of what constitutes achievement for women is more complex. Most of the literature on achievement and on fear of failure has assumed, either explicitly or implicitly, that "achievement" is comprised of accomplishments that have been traditionally thought of as male in nature: success in work or academic settings (in many studies fear of failure is defined as test anxiety), tasks that are done independently, priorities that follow one's own bent instead of being concerned with pleasing or taking care of others. Contemporary views of women's development challenge this notion. They suggest that achievement for women is not simply an accomplishment in the traditional domain of work or *individual* effort. Rather, achievement for women incorporates the domain of interpersonal affiliation, and therefore commitment in a relationship and the establishment and maintenance of intimacy are also valued.

Clinical Manifestations

Clinically, fear of failure can present as a glaring problem, but more often, it is subtle and difficult to detect. In their discussion of procrastination, Burka and Yuen (1983) delineated several indicators of fear of failure, the most prominent of which is perfectionism. Perfectionistic thinking is clearly evident when a woman says or behaves in ways consistent with the belief, "I can never make a mistake" or "If I'm not number 1, then I'm nothing." A constant sense of guilt, self-recrimination, and lament may characterize a woman who fears not being perfect. Perfectionism can also play a role in indecisiveness (a fear that she will not make the right decision), the inability to make a commitment, the intolerance of being in a position of not knowing or not understanding, and the attempt to do everything. The perfectionistic woman may have trouble saying no to requests from others, since that could mean she has limitations and therefore is not perfect. She may insist that she cannot be "mediocre" or "ordinary," and she may avoid or sabotage competitive efforts, fearing that she will lose.

One of the more subtle signs of fear of failure is an attitude of apathy or disinterest about an endeavor. A woman may devalue some area of her life, insisting that she doesn't really care about it. In reality, the longing and loss she experiences around this are so profound that she must deny it altogether. Similarly, it may be hard to detect fear of failure in the woman who "does it all," especially if she is very successful. Embodying the ideal contemporary woman, she manages career, family, and a dazzling array of interests and activities, yet she may be driven by a secret terror that if she does anything less she will have failed. It is common for a successful woman who fears failure to feel that she is a fraud, and that it is only a matter of time before her deception is discovered.

FEAR OF FAILURE: THE LITERATURE

Fear of failure has been addressed in the literature from a number of different conceptual frameworks. Achievement motivation theorists have researched fear of failure as one of the two primary motives of the need for achievement, the other being "Hope for Success" (McClelland, Atkinson, Clark & Lowell, 1953). Birney, Burdick, and Teevan (1969) have compiled a thorough review of this literature, and interested readers are referred to their book for a comprehensive discussion of this work. The motive to avoid failure was posited to be a major factor in those people who seemed to be apprehensive, cautious, and often irrational in achievement-related settings (Hancock & Teevan, 1964), who evidenced either low self-confidence or extreme optimism about their personal qualifications, or who showed puzzling discrepancies between level of aspiration and performance (Birney et al., 1969). Such people performed poorly on competitive tasks, but did better in a cooperative situation. After failing at a task, they often became apathetic or defensive, tried to leave the field, devalued the task as unimportant or uninteresting, or claimed that they hadn't really tried (Birney et al., 1969).

Birney et al. (1969) have suggested that the person who fears failure does not want to feel *responsible* for the nonattainment of a goal because this would lead to a lowering of the self-estimate. "Nonattainment is experienced as failure *when it is accepted as evidence that the self-estimate has been higher than it ought to be*. When this happens, the self-estimate is lowered and the process of lowering one's evaluation is experienced as failure" (p. 202, original italics). These authors also note that fear of failure may be a function of fear of losing social approval or of the reality consequences of failure. Unfortunately, their research was conducted entirely with men, so it is difficult to say how generalizable their results are for women.

Some attribution theorists would agree with the emphasis on self-esteem as the foundation for the problem of fear of failure (Beery, 1975; Covington & Beery, 1976; Covington & Omelich, 1984). They suggest that there is an essential link between a person's perceived level of ability and his or her feelings of self-worth. Because ability is viewed as a prime ingredient for success, and inability as a major cause of failure, "the perceived instrumental value of ability makes the protection of a sense of competency of the highest priority—higher sometimes than even achievement itself" (Covington & Omelich, 1984, p. 160). Thus, the fear of failure motivation is a function not only of external consequences, as suggested by Teevan and McGhee (1972), but also of a competing need: the protection of a sense of competence (Covington & Omelich, 1984, p. 162).

Beery (1975) and Burka and Yuen (1983) have explicated the relationship between self-esteem, ability, and performance. Beery (1975) observed that students often make the following set of assumptions: (1) What I produce is a direct reflection of my ability level; (2) My ability level determines how worthwhile I am as a person; therefore, (3) What I produce is a reflection of my worth as a person. These assumptions form the equation:

Self-worth = Ability = Performance

Burka and Yuen (1983) applied Beery's self-worth equation in examining the relationship between fear of failure and procrastination. They note that ability can be defined in many different ways, and that a problem arises when ability (and hence, performance) becomes the *sole* determinant of self-worth. When this is the case, every performance or task becomes the total measure of the person: "An outstanding performance means an outstanding person; a mediocre performance means a mediocre person" (Burka & Yuen, 1983, p. 21). Procrastination, they suggest, is one way for people to protect the sense of ability (competence) and self-worth, since a disappointing performance can be attributed to lack of effort rather than to lack of ability. People who fear failure often avoid any true test of their ability, not allowing their performance to be an accurate reflection of their level of ability (Berry, 1975; Burka & Yuen, 1983; Covington & Omelich, 1984; Covington & Berry, 1976).

There are several limitations in the existing literature in the domain of achievement theory. Most of these studies do not examine individual differences and their relation to character structure, which are essential concerns for the clinician. For example, there is no distinction between responses of subjects who are neurotic from those who are borderline or narcissistic. Another major problem is that very little of this research has been done with women, or has been designed to delineate the differences between men and women with respect to fear of failure and achievement. Matina Horner (1972) addressed this question in her groundbreaking work on achievement-related conflicts in women, postulating that it is the motive to avoid success, not fear of failure, that is a primary factor in women's work inhibitions. Although her work has been debated, her finding that women often view success as interfering with relationships is notable. This observation is in accord with Hoffman (1974), who found that while the content of men's fears focuses on the questioning of the value of the achievement, women consistently fear affiliative loss.

Although Horner and Hoffman focused their work on women's fears, we think it is unfortunate that they nevertheless conceptualized achievement only in what are traditionally masculine terms, i.e., accomplishment in the world of work and individual effort. New views of women's development, deriving primarily from the contemporary socio-psychological and psychoanalytic literature, suggest that making relationships work is also an important achievement for women. Fear of success, defined by Horner in part as fear of loss of femininity, and described by some as "fear of deviance" (e.g., Person, 1982), means in essence that a woman is afraid of being less feminine or being seen as less feminine. We would suggest that this is tantamount to "failure," for if a woman succeeds in the domain of individual/career accomplishment, she may feel that she has failed "as a woman." Thus, we would agree with those who have suggested that fear of failure and fear of success are, for women, essentially equivalent (e.g., Stein & Bailey, 1973; Steinberg, Teevan & Greenfeld, 1983).

Fear of failure has also been addressed in the psychoanalytic literature, usually in the context of work or academic inhibitions. The traditional view, one that is still held by a part of the analytic community (e.g., Chehrazi, 1986; Lampl de Groot, 1982), is that fear of failure in women is a symptom of underlying penis envy. Because of their lack of a penis (and the associated social power, status, and mobility that has long been accorded men in western cultures), women are seen as inferior to men. They may present therapy with "a general doubt as to their capacities, even to the point of conviction that some essential feature necessary for success is missing" (Applegarth, 1976, p. 256).

Understandably, there have been many criticisms of this classical view over the years. Feminists have stated that if women do experience penis envy, it is because they have been denied power by patriarchal forces which dominate our culture. Further, they claim that it is inappropriate to apply Freud's original conceptualization to women because it is based on a model of male development which regards femininity as a secondary, rather than a primary, identification.

Both the classical psychoanalytic view and its feminist critique are problematic in that they are limited conceptually. Penis envy only refers to oedipal-level conflicts and does not address pre-oedipal issues (e.g., separation-individuation). Additionally, penis envy may not be the best understanding of the oedipal conflict for girls. Feminist critiques tend to focus on external, cultural factors and often overlook internal psychodynamics. Further, like most motivation theorists, most feminists and psychoanalytic theorists conceptualize achievement in male terms, without considering what achievement is for women.

FEMALE DEVELOPMENT, ACHIEVEMENT, AND THE FEAR OF FAILURE

We would like to propose that to understand the concept of achievement for women and its concomitant problems, such as fear of failure, it is necessary to take into account the domains of individual accomplishment and interpersonal affiliation while simultaneously considering female development, cultural variables (contemporary values and gender role socialization), and the individual's life history and character structure. Since a woman's sense of herself centers around her connections to others (Gilligan, 1982), to address only individual accomplishment is to ignore an essential component of women's psychology which is distinctly different from that of men. As Miller (1983) proposes, feminine development is characterized by phases of an increasingly complex sense of self in the context of relationships. This sense of self reflects the motivation to develop and maintain connections to both interpersonal relations and intrapsychic representations. Thus, if we are to understand fear of failure in women we have a complex task.

The close relationship between achievement and affiliation for women has been addressed by many authors (e.g., Gilligan, 1982; Hoffman, 1972, 1974; Jackaway & Teevan, 1976; Stein & Bailey, 1973). They have emphasized that women's conflicts about achievement are strongly influenced by socialized gender-appropriate behaviors. While a woman's pursuit of excellence may be motivated by an internalized standard of excellence, the areas of achievement are determined by cultural values of what is feminine (Person, 1982; Stein & Bailey, 1973). In addition, we see fear of failure manifested in conflicts about intimacy. Because social relationships are "women's work," an inability to achieve one's expectations for close, intimate relationships and/ or a viable social network can also be experienced as failure.

Our understanding of feminine development is expanded by the newer psychoanalytic literature (Chessick, 1984; Chodorow, 1978; Clower, 1979; Notman, Zilbach, Baker-Miller & Nadelson, 1986; Kanefield, 1985a, 1985b; Person, 1982). No longer espousing a phallocentric view emphasizing castration and penis envy, these authors emphasize the complex identification of a girl with her mother and her fear of loss of love. Notman and her colleagues (1986) suggest that female development can best be understood as a separate line of development based on "female body awareness, identification with the mother, and cognitive development as organizers" (p. 247). As women (mothers) are not afforded the same value as men socioculturally, females are identifying with a cultural negative. An unconscious identification with a devalued maternal figure results in low self-esteem (Person, 1982). Person (1982) believes that the major underlying dynamic in women's inhibitions is not penis envy, but fear of loss of love. She questions whether the female tendency toward affiliation is based on cultural values and role expectations, or is related to the developmental sequence of female object relations.

There is a debate within the psychoanalytic literature as to the source of the female investment in relational ties. Chodorow (1978) provides an extensive review of the literature and concludes that girls have a more difficult time during separation-individuation than boys, because of the mother's view of the daughter as a narcissistic extension of herself. Person (1982) takes a different view, emphasizing the oedipal constellation for girls. She notes that since the girl's erotic rival is also the source of dependent gratification, the turn to the father is experienced as a loss. Person (1982) states that it is the girl's ambivalence toward her mother which is "the central dynamic in female sexual inhibition, the all pervasive dread of loss of love, and work inhibitions" (p. 82).

We would suggest that a successful resolution of this conflict is a difficult task. The girl must maintain a tie to mother for the fulfillment of dependency needs, while simultaneously choosing father (males) as the preferred libinidal object. In maintaining an exclusive or preferential tie to her mother, a daughter must deny her full development as a woman. On the other hand, by choosing father and moving on with her life, a daughter may fear that she has failed her mother by abandoning her.

The resolution of the preoedipal and/or oedipal conflicts are never perfect, and fear of failure may prove to be a consequence. This is more likely to occur when either the girl's mother or father has conflicts which interfere with encouraging their daughter in her development. In an effort to maintain the tie to her mother, a daughter may sacrifice her work goals and/or her love life. If the conflict is primarily preoedipal, the daughter must never separate psychologically from her mother. This may take the form of "never growing up" or growing up to become the mother's idealized conception of herself. If, on the other had, the conflict is primarily oedipal, the daughter must never compete too successfully with her mother, either in her experience of work or love.

There has been support in the literature for these ideas. For example, Halpern (1964) examined the familial relationships of academically inhibited children and adolescents and found disturbances in both preoedipal and oedipal issues. In families with controlling, narcissistic parents, the children resorted to extreme measures (school failure) to achieve individuation from the parent(s). Where familial relationships intensified the children's oedipal conflict, the children expressed themselves negativistically and passively. Hellman (1959) observed narcissistically intrusive mothers who demanded that their children sacrifice their own realities to their mothers', which often resulted in low self-esteem and work inhibition.

In addition to these developmental issues, we must now consider the relationship between fear of failure and individual differences in character structure. For example, the aspect of fear of failure which is usually of primary concern for neurotic clients is fear of the loss of the object's love. For narcissistic clients (ranging from "healthy" to "severely impaired"), the primary concern is the loss of the idealized, grandiose self or the idealized other. For borderline clients, the experience of failure is tantamount to the fragmentation of the self and to the loss of the good (part) object.[1] For women with narcissistic-masochistic character structures, described by Cooper (1986), fear of failure may be the core conflict around which all else revolves, and almost every encounter in the world is experienced in terms of failure or success.

It is important to understand the concepts of narcissism and masochism more fully because they bear a special relation to fear of failure. Baker (1979) has examined the relationship between academic failure and the narcissistic character structure. In Baker's conceptualization, the grandiose self in narcissistic individuals leads to academic failure because students are unable to avoid the frustration and small failures which occur in the normal learning process. Such "failures" are experienced as narcissistic injuries, so studies are avoided and other activities are defensively pursued in order to maintain the inflated, grandiose self.

The pursuit of failure and discomfort are also discussed by Schafer (1984) and Cooper (1986). Each provides a clinical profile of masochism which bears directly on the experience of fear of failure. Schafer notes, like Baker (1979), that the experience of failure results in the comparison between an extravagant ideal self and the real self. He expands the context to include a severe superego with respect to which every pleasure must be paid for with painful quilt and self-destruction, and suffering itself is sexualized. This discrepancy between what is expected, what is experienced (or anticipated), and the resulting self-punishment is the report of our clients paralyzed by fear of failure. Fear of failure may be a form of masochism, in that the constant sense of inadequacy which underlies fear of failure is, in one sense, a perpetuation of pain and suffering. Cooper's (1986) concept of the narcissistic-masochist provides the outline of an individual pursuing defeat and victimization, who is unable to experience pleasure, and is consumed by self-centered suffering. With success this person is riddled with guilt and depression; likewise with failure this individual is depressed. The narcissistic-masochist may be the most challenging client to present with fear of failure. Although tormented by her conflicts, often regarding

both intimacy and individual accomplishment, this client experiences discomfort with both success and failure. As it is through
suffering and victimization that this client knows herself, success
in treatment is hard won.

In summary, to understand fear of failure in women it is necessary to integrate what have previously been conceptualized as
separate domains: individual accomplishment and interpersonal
affiliation. A woman's personal experience of failure and of success (and her fear thereof) occurs in the context of both domains.
The realm of individual accomplishment has best been investigated by achievement-motivation and attribution theorists. The
findings that are most salient for our discussion are: (1) there is a
fundamental relationship between fear of failure and self-worth;
(2) the experience of failure derives from a discrepancy between
what a person expects and how s/he perceives what s/he has
achieved; (3) the protection of self-worth and a sense of competence often take precedence over the effort to achieve successfully; and (4) efforts to preserve self-worth and competence can
range from underachievement to overachievement. The importance of interpersonal affiliation for women has best been illumi-
nated by the new psychoanalytic conceptualizations of female
development. This theoretical conceptualization clarifies why
women's achievement is rooted in affiliation. The central dynamic in women's inhibitions is the ambivalence toward the
mother. This brings with it the dread of loss of love, which lays
the groundwork for fear of failure. A related notion from the
psychoanalytic perspective is that fear of failure exists when
there is a discrepancy between the ideal self and the real self.
With narcissistic-masochism, there exist both this discrepancy
and a severe superego which prevents or punishes every pleasure
and accomplishment.

CLINICAL EXAMPLES

What follows are brief clinical vignettes which illustrate fear
of failure in neurotic, narcissistic, borderline, and narcissistic-
masochistic clients. In each diagnostic category, the severity of
symptoms can range from mild to severe. We hope that these

examples provide the reader an opportunity to follow our thinking about fear of failure in women.

When the neurotic client is inhibited by fear of failure, this inhibition is likely to be in either the domain of accomplishment or intimacy. Further, it is unlikely that this inhibition will markedly impair her life. We will present two examples of neurotic clients. In the first vignette, the client suffers an inhibition in the domain of intimacy. In the second, the client is inhibited in her work.

Ms. N. consulted a therapist for problems in her relationship with her husband. A pleasant young woman, her interpersonal efforts with all friends, co-workers, family and husband were based on her efforts to please, placate, and keep everything smooth and happy. Although she reported that she and her husband "adored each other," she had been unable to achieve an orgasm with intercourse throughout their 15-year marriage. She is only able to achieve an orgasm when masturbating with a fantasy of debasement and humiliation. What is most troubling to her is her experience that she is failing as a woman and in her relationship to her husband. She has never told him her experience for fear of becoming unworthy of his love.

Ms. T. is a college professor in her late 30s, who is happily married with two young children. She is warm, gracious, and well-liked by students and colleagues who also respect her intelligence, creativity, and dedication to her work. Although she sought treatment for what she called "procrastination," it was evident that she didn't actually have a problem doing her work. In fact, she loved to work and she worked hard, but she constantly felt that she had not done enough and should work even harder. The problem was that she worked too hard. She once described how she overprepared for the undergraduate lectures she gave, reading numerous original sources for every class because she was afraid that a student might ask a question that she couldn't answer. Not being able to answer a question meant that she had failed to fulfill her part in the student-teacher relationship. As a result of such overwork, she didn't have as much time as she needed to do her own research and writing, and her upcoming tenure application was in jeopardy.

The narcissistic client without masochistic features is one, not surprisingly, that we have seen less frequently in our practices. Our hypothesis is that these people are more likely to be successful at work but have more difficulty with intimacy. Highly defended, the better functioning narcissist rarely comes for therapy on her own.

Ms. M., a 45 year-old divorced mother of two teenagers, is a very successful businesswoman. Bright and articulate, she holds her own in the board room. Her lover initiated couple's therapy because she consistently avoided marriage. The couple's therapist referred her for individual treatment, finding her "impossible to work with." What became readily apparent was Ms. M.'s pattern of devaluation. Bright, successful suitors became flawed mates to be avoided. She would string them along, receiving expensive gifts, while repelling their wishes for closeness. Her "perfection" was preserved as long as she was pursued by men valued by others. Intimacy endangered her carefully constructed sense of perfect self-sufficiency. Not surprisingly, she left individual therapy prematurely when the therapist "failed to be perfect."

The borderline client is more likely to show inhibitions in both external achievement as well as intimacy, and these inhibitions are likely to be of greater severity than in the neurotic or narcissistic patient.

Ms. B., a 33 year-old assistant vice-president of finance for a large technology firm, was referred for therapy by the company employee assistance program. She was profoundly anxious and depressed, having procrastinated on her work for so long that she feared losing her job as soon as it was discovered how little she had been doing. She had built up an excellent reputation, and it was of great importance to her that she was known as someone who never made a mistake; this seemed to her to be the one attribute that led other people to value her. If she made an error, she felt, her world would crumble. The precipitant for her procrastination and depression was the fact that she had recently been assigned to a new project and, as to be expected, she didn't know everything perfectly. Rather than propelling her toward mastery, however, the experience of not knowing everything paralyzed her. She could hardly get out of bed in the morning and could do little more than sit in her office and stare at the walls during the day. In the domain of intimacy, this woman evidenced major inhibitions: she did not date nor did she have any friends. Indeed, she avoided anything more than perfunctory conversations with people because she was terrified they would ask her something personal and, having nothing to say, she would show them what a "nothing person" she was. The youngest of three children, she lived at home with her widowed mother, bound in a relationship of mutual resentment and dependency from which she could not extricate herself. Her guilt about her anger prevented her from leaving her mother.

The narcissistic-masochist, depending on her level of development, may have inhibitions in one or both domains of work and intimacy, reflecting the full range of severity. The client in the first vignette is severely impaired. The second client is very well adapted.

Ms. Q. is a 30 year-old divorced woman. Dressing as a mismatched 15 year-old waif and speaking with a constant whine, she presents herself as the helpless victim in both her work and personal life. Employed in a technical position far below her aspirations and abilities, she constantly bemoans that it is too late for her to catch up and make anything of her life. Although very bright, she has never fulfilled her own expectations to be a child prodigy and has only fallen further and further behind her aspirations with each passing year. Frightened of pursuing her potential because she may fall short, she constricts herself to busywork. Her efforts at work result in her grinding away endlessly on tasks she describes as "grunt work." She is constantly overlooked for promotions or raises. She is known for her competence on tasks requiring attention to detail, her lack of imagination, and her lack of self-initiation. She is shunned by co-workers, as they find her touchy and difficult. Her personal relationships are no more satisfying. She avoids and/or provokes others to shun her out of her fears of exploitation and victimization. This is best captured by her interactions with the therapist, whom she attempts to provoke to anger. She devalues both the therapist and the therapeutic work. For example, the client accuses the therapist of not helping enough and of feigning interest solely to receive the fee. She reports with a mixture of venom and delight that the therapist is easily bought. Additionally, she accuses the therapist of taking advantage of her by charging for something that should be provided simply out of love. This provocation is motivated by the client's fear of failing in this most highly valued intimate relationship. If she were to care about the work and the therapist, she risks the possibility that her love for the therapist will be deemed unworthy.

A successful and well-regarded mental health professional sought treatment because she was unhappy with her current love relationship. She had had a string of unsatisfying relationships with people whom she experienced as being emotionally unavailable. She often felt unjustly deprived because she gave so much time, attention, and support to her partners without getting the same in return. In fact, she provided the emotional glue which held her relationships together. Despite this, her explanation of her partners' unavailability was that something was wrong with her: she was too demanding, too intrusive, too withholding, too fat, too needy, too smart, too dumb, etc. Although she selected inadequate partners, she made herself the failure. This protected her from pursuing appropriate relationships in which there was a real possibility that she would fail. Although she had numerous close friends and a strong support network, she secretly felt abandoned and unappreciated, doomed to suffer and endure this injustice alone.

CONCLUSION

Currently, there is a great deal of discussion about fear of failure and women's conflicts about achievement. A review of the literature and examination of the issues involved leads us to conclude, as have others, that fear of failure is not a simple unidimensional construct.

For women, fear of failure encompasses two major domains: individual accomplishment and interpersonal affiliation. Women can be afraid to fail in either of these two major areas of life: work and love. We believe that these ideas have important clinical implications. Until fear of failure can be moderated, a woman who fears that she isn't or won't be good enough will not be able to take pleasure in living. A model for understanding the full range and complexity of fear of failure has been presented in this paper. With a more informed understanding of fear of failure, we can, hopefully, help our clients free themselves of the internal burden of the impossible search for perfection and the terror of perpetually falling short.

NOTE

1. As may be obvious to the reader, we have drawn on the theoretical language provided by both Kohut and Kernberg. It is beyond the scope of this paper to discuss fully the differences in their conceptualizations of borderline and narcissistic characters. We refer the reader to Kernberg's *Serve Personality Disorders* (1984) and to Kohut's *Analysis of the Self* (1971).

REFERENCES

Applegarth, A. (1976) Some observations on work inhibitions in women. *Journal of the American Psychoanalytic Association, 24*, 251-268.
Baker, H. (1979) The conquering hero quits: Narcissistic factors in underachievement and failure. *American Journal of Psychotherapy, 23*(3), 418-427.
Beery, R. (1975) Fear of failure in the student experience. *The Personnel and Guidance Journal, 54*, 190-203.
Birney, R., Burdick, H. and Teevan, R. (1969) *Fear of failure*, New York: Van Nostrand-Reinhold Co.

Burka, J. and Yuen, L. (1983) *Procrastination: Why you do it, what to do about it*, Reading, MA: Addison-Wesley.

Chehrazi, S. (1986) Female psychology: A review. *Journal of the American Psychoanalytic Association, 34*(1), 141-162.

Chessick, R. (1984) Was Freud wrong about feminine psychology? *American Journal of Psychoanalysis, 44*(4), 355-367.

Chodorow, N. (1978) *The reproduction of mothering: Psychoanalysis and the sociology of gender*, Berkeley, CA: University of California Press.

Clower, V. (1979) Feminism and the new psychology of women. In Karasu, R. and Socarides, C. (eds.), *On sexuality*, New York: International Universities Press, Inc., 279-315.

Cooper, A. (1986) Masochism as character trait. Paper presented at Masochism Symposium, San Francisco, CA.

Covington, M. and Beery, R. (1976) *Self-worth and school learning*, New York: Holt, Reinhart, and Winston.

Covington, M. and Omelich, C. (1984) Controversies or consistencies? A reply to Brown and Weiner. *Journal of Educational Psychology, 76*(1), 159-168.

Gilligan, C. (1982) *In a different voice*, Cambridge, MA: Harvard University Press.

Halpern, H. (1964) Psychodynamic and cultural determinants of work inhibition in children and adolescents. *Psychoanalytic Review, 51*, 173-189.

Hancock, J. and Teevan, R. (1964) Fear of failure and risk-taking behavior. *Journal of Personality, 32*, 200-209.

Hellman, I. (1954) Some observations on mothers of children with intellectual inhibitions. *Psychoanalytic Study of the Child, 9*, 259-274.

Hoffman, L. (1972) Early childhood experiences and women's achievement motives. *Journal of Social Issues, 28*(2), 129-155.

Hoffman, L. (1974) Fear of success in males and females: 1965 and 1971. *Journal of Consulting and Clinical Psychology, 42*(3), 353-358.

Horner, M. (1972) Toward an understanding of achievement-related conflicts in women. *Journal of Social Issues, 28*(2), 157-175.

Jackaway, R. and Teevan, R. (1976) Fear of failure and fear of success: Two dimensions of the same motive. *Sex Roles, 2*(3), 283-293.

Kancfield, L. (1985a) Psychoanalytic constructions of female development and women's conflicts about achievement. Part I. *Journal of the American Academy of Psychoanalysis, 13*(2), 229-246.

Kancfield, L. (1985b) Psychoanalytic constructions of female development and women's conflicts about achievement. Part II. *Journal of the American Academy of Psychoanalysis, 13*(3), 347-366.

Kernberg, O. *Severe personality disorders*, New Haven: Yale University Press.

Kohut, H. (1971) *Analysis of the self, Vol. 1*, New York: International Universities Press.

Lampl de Groot, J. (1982) Thoughts on psychoanalytic views of female psychology. *Psychoanalytic Quarterly, 51*(1), 1-18.

McClelland, D., Atkinson, J., Clark, R. and Lowell, E. (1953) *The achievement motive*, New York: Appleton-Century-Crofts.

Miller, J. (1983) The development of women's sense of self. Conference on Women's Emerging Identity, American Academy of Psychoanalysis, as cited by Notman et al. (1986) Themes in psychoanalytic understanding of women: Some reconsiderations of autonomy and affiliation. *Journal of the American Academy of Psychoanalysis, 14*(2), 241-253.

Notman, M., Zelbach, J., Baker-Miller, J. and Nadelson, C. (1986) Themes in psychoanalytic understanding of women: Some reconsiderations of autonomy and affiliation. *Journal of the American Academy of Psychoanalysis, 14*(2), 241-253.

Person, E. (1982) Women working: Fears of failure, deviance, and success. *Journal of the American Academy of Psychoanalysis, 10*(1), 67-84.

Schafer, R. (1984) The pursuit of failure and the idealization of unhappiness. *American Psychologist, 39*(4), 398-405.

Stein, A. and Bailey, M. (1973) Socialization of achievement orientation in females. *Psychological Bulletin, 80*(5), 345-366.

Steinberg, C., Teevan, R. and Greenfeld, N. (1983) Sex-role orientation and fear of failure in women. *Psychological Reports, 52*, 987-992.

Teevan, R. and McGhee, P. (1972) Childhood development of fear of failure motivation. *Journal of Personality and Social Psychology, 21*(3), 345-348.

"I Know This Is Stupid, but . . ."
Or, Some Thoughts on Why Female
Students Fear Failure
and Not Success

Carla Golden

Women's so-called fear of success has been widely discussed and disputed. One can find numerous references to it in the Psychological Abstracts, psychology of women textbooks, and review articles. In contrast, references to women's fear of failure are not as readily found in the psychological literature. What is intriguing to me about all the attention give to women's fear of success, is that in my experience as a teacher who frequently deals with women students and their fears, I have found fears of failure to figure far more prominently in their personal concerns than fears of success.

For nine years, I have been teaching and talking primarily with female students, first at a private women's college and then at a private coeducational institution where 80% of psychology majors (and hence students in my classes) are women. Thus, my intent here is not to compare the fears of female and male students, but to consider the content of women's expressed fears, specifically as they relate to success or failure. If I were to characterize the nature of these fears, most would fall into the category of fear of failure rather than fear of success. Such fears of failure could further be classified into two broad categories: fears

Carla Golden, PhD, is Associate Professor in the Department of Psychology at Ithaca College. She is an active member of the Association for Women in Psychology and has written and lectured on topics related to sexuality, gender, and object relations theory.

pertaining to academic or intellectual failure and fears pertaining to interpersonal failure.

One prominent form of fear of failure is manifested in the classroom by female students who are reluctant to express opinions for fear of appearing unintelligent. The reason I know that this is what often underlies the silence which not infrequently follows my request for comments is that when the silence remains unbroken, my response has been to ask students to tell me what thoughts (if any) are going through their minds at that moment. At first, I had thought that the silent students were not thinking about anything relevant to the questions I had posed, but were merely waiting for their more talkative classmates to respond. What I have learned however, is that many of them had formulated responses, but were not willing to expose them in front of the class for fear of "looking stupid."

The same fear of appearing unintelligent seems to affect the likelihood of a student asking a question in class. Despite repeated assurances that I appreciate questions during class, I am not as often asked to explain something in class as I am approached privately after class. When a student does take the risk of spontaneously asking a question or making a statement in class, she will not uncommonly preface her remarks with the comment, "I know this is stupid, but. . . ." In my classroom experience, this remark occurs with disturbing frequency.

In contrast to the many students who have explicitly acknowledged the fear of appearing intellectually incompetent, I have never had a student who explained her classroom silence in terms of the fear of appearing too intelligent. Perhaps this would be more common in classes with a higher percentage of male students, or perhaps women students do in fact feel this way but are reluctant to admit it. While students have told me that they "know women who are like that," never have I known a student to identify herself as one of them. On the basis of such observations one might conclude that fear of failure, in the form of appearing stupid, is more common than fear of success, in the form of appearing smart, or alternatively that the latter fear is the more difficult to acknowledge, and hence the more profound.

Included within the category of fear of academic failure would be student concerns about performance in graduate school. I have known more than a few young women who are afraid they will fail to perform competently; among them are very bright students whose high levels of undergraduate success might serve as the basis for feeling confident about their ability to do graduate work. These young women are classic exemplars of the imposter phenomenon (Clance and Imes, 1978).

In contrast, I have known only a few students who I would characterize as fearing success in graduate school, and even in these cases it was not a fear of success per se, but of the consequences of graduate school attendance on other aspects of their lives, specifically existing intimate relationships, or the probability of establishing them. What I have observed to be much more common (and this is something I would definitely not categorize as indicative of a fear of success), is the number of young women who have made the conscious and deliberate choice to avoid demanding graduate school programs because they wanted to pursue careers which would allow the time and flexibility necessary for a lifestyle in which family commitments were primary.

For example, I have spoken with some very bright and academically successful students who want to work as therapists, and who decide to enroll in social work programs as opposed to clinical psychology graduate programs. This is not because they anticipate a greater likelihood of acceptance or more success in social work school, or alternatively because they anticipate a lower probability of acceptance or the greater possibility of failure in a clinical psychology program, but because they don't want to spend five years in school and/or training at a time when they wish to be pursuing marriage and family possibilities. These students have considered what they see as their options and have made "choices." While one might legitimately question the notion of choice within a patriarchal society and regret that women's career aspirations have sometimes suffered as a result, it is not the case that these women fear success. Rather, they do not seek it in its male defined terms.

From my experience as a teacher, I have seen evidence of women's fears of academic and intellectual failure, both in terms of classroom behavior and in anticipated graduate school performance. It is worth noting that with regard to how students see themselves in relation to the occupational world, I do not commonly hear much about fears of either failure or success. Concern seems to center more specifically on what occupational field to pursue and whether or not one will be able to find satisfying and enjoyable work within that field.

Among my women students fears of failure within the interpersonal realm are far more common than fears of academic failure. Such fears take a variety of different expressions. One that is common among first year students is the fear of failing to make close friends. This fear is one where I have some basis for making a comparison between male and female students. This semester, I am teaching a large introductory psychology class, and on the first day of class I handed out index cards on which I asked the students to write various bits of personal information, including some of the things that they looked forward to in their college years, and some things that they were apprehensive about. Relevant to the current discussion were their apprehensions.

Female students were only slightly more likely than their male peers to express concerns about doing well in school (e.g., not being able to keep up with the work and/or getting poor grades). They were, however, much more likely than male students to express concern about making friends. For example, one student expressed the concerns of a significant minority when she wrote, "I'm really worried that I won't be able to make the kind of close friends that I had in high school and that I'll be lonely here."

That female students were more likely to express fear of failure in developing close friendships does not suggest to me that they will actually have greater difficulty establishing friendships. Rather, their ability to explicitly identify this concern indicates that they are well aware of the value that friendship plays in their lives. Implicit in their written comments was an acknowledgment that forming friendships was important to their well being and that if they failed in this realm they would be failing themselves. This was the one kind of fear of interpersonal failure where their own needs seemed to figure most prominently.

Another commonly expressed fear among women students is the fear of failing other people, and often the desire not to fail others means that their own needs are given less priority. Over and over again, I have spoken to female students who are afraid that they are failing their friends, their parents, their boyfriends, and occasionally, their teachers. A common theme is articulated by students who are unable to do their schoolwork when a friend is upset and needs to talk. One student who had sustained a serious physical injury which often left her tired and unable to concentrate, felt that she had to expend what little energy she had listening to her friends, rather than studying for an upcoming exam. Upon failing the exam, this same student expressed the concern that she had failed me (there was no mention of having failed herself).

Another variation on this same theme involves students who are unable to seek the support they desperately need from parents because they don't want to disappoint or disturb them. I have known three students to withhold from their mothers the fact that they were raped because it would be "devastating" to them. In other cases, they are unable to speak honestly with their parents about their academic problems in school, or about sexuality issues. Many of these students explicitly express that they can't go to their parents for support because to do so would be to "disappoint" or "fail" them.

I have listened to many an instance where a boyfriend's needs are put before one's own. One particularly interesting case involved a young woman who had been asked out by two men who were roommates. She was fond of each man, and wanted to keep dating both of them, but the situation was creating friction between the two roommates. She came to me with her problem and told me that what she had decided to do was not go out with either of them. Though this would deny her the pleasure of their company, she felt that it would solve their problem. It hadn't occurred to this otherwise sensible woman that by so doing she was not taking herself and her own needs as seriously as she was taking theirs.

I have provided a very brief sketch of the kinds of fears of failure expressed by some of my women students. Such concerns do not necessarily characterize a majority of my students, nor do they constitute the entire range of things that they fear. Some of the more common fears include fear of controversy, of nuclear war, of what other people will think of them, of continued inequality for women, of having to make difficult decisions that others might not like, of being raped, of being "real" (i.e., open and honest) with their parents, etc. But I would not characterize these as fundamentally involving fear of failing. I mention them so that my focus in this paper on fears of failure does not leave the reader with a distorted sense that the young women with whom I've talked fear only failure.

There are two issues related to the fear of failure in women students which I would like to briefly address. One concerns whether such fears are seriously problematic and detrimental for those who express them. Directly connected to this is how I, as an educator rather than a therapist, deal with these fears when they are presented or when I see them manifested. It is not entirely obvious whether the existence of a fear directly affects behavior. I have known students who have doubted their ability to perform successfully in graduate school, but this has not deterred them from attending and from achieving high levels of success. On the other hand, it is fairly clear that a student who fears appearing unintelligent and thus chooses not to voice her views is losing the opportunity to express herself and to (potentially) learn from experience that others do not see her as intellectually inferior.

In the interpersonal realm, when a woman expresses a fear of failing to meet the needs of others, what this may indicate is not that she is likely to fail to do so, but that she values this ability in herself, is willing to work to avoid failing, and can use her eventual success as a basis for positive self-definition. I am not unaware that this tendency to put the needs of other people first has worked against women's awareness of, and attention to, their own needs; I am merely being sensitive to (and thus trying to avoid) the tendency to pathologize women's behavior and/or to focus on its problematic aspects.

As a teacher, I am in a rather different position than a therapist with regard to dealing with student fears of failure. The student-teacher relationship is much less structured and clearly defined than that between a therapist and client. If a student does not acknowledge and/or experience her fear as problematic, and does not seek my assistance in dealing with it, what is my responsibility in pointing it out to her? Among those students who do come to in my office, some are directly seeking advice or assistance, but others merely want someone to listen to them. While I react to each student on an individual basis, there is a general rule I apply when a student presents or manifests fear of failure concerns. Whether it be a reluctance to speak out in class, imposter feelings, or a fear of disappointing some significant other, I share with students my observation of how the same fears exist among their female peers. I want them to know that they are not alone in feeling the way they do, that gender based socialization contributes to their common experience, and in the case of fear of failure in meeting the needs of others, that it is critical to include their own needs among those requiring attention.

On the basis of my experience as a teacher who frequently deals with the concerns of female students, I have found more evidence of the fear of failure (both academic and interpersonal) than I have of the fear of success. This has led me to wonder why it is the latter which is so much more frequently researched and referred to in the psychological literature than the former.

The power of naming and the corresponding invisibility of that which is not named must be at least partially responsible for the continued focus on fear of success. Research on the topic was most prevalent in the early and mid seventies, but even today it receives major coverage in psychology of women textbooks and in the psychological literature. Despite all the attention to the topic there is still controversy regarding the existence of gender differences in fear of success. Two recent review articles provide rather different assessments on the state of the research with regard to this point.

Henley (1985), in a Signs review essay on Psychology and Gender, considers fear of success to be a phenomenon that captured public attention but could not withstand the scrutiny of careful scholarly investigation. Henley cites Tresemer's (1977) review of the research on the topic and attributes to it the conclusion that "there is no significant difference between females and males in the incidence of FOS imagery" (p. 104). In contrast, Sutherland and Veroff (1985), in an article on "Achievement Motivation and Sex Roles," review the same literature, and conclude that most studies have shown fear of success to be "valid and meaningful only for females" (p. 109). In direct opposition to Henley's claim, they conclude that Tresemer's review of the research supports the assertion that "fear of success has been generally found to be more frequent in females" (p. 109). While both reviews tend to agree that the differences have never been found to be as large as those originally reported by Horner (1968), their overall conclusions are at odds with one another, and reflect the continuing controversy over the construct of fear of success.

Despite such continuing debate, the notion of women's fear of success has gained popular currency. The extent to which this idea has become so firmly incorporated into many people's thinking about women and achievement is remarkable. Many of my students believe it to be a well established and accepted aspect of women's psychology, though I have rarely known a student to find the concept meaningful as an explanation of her own behavior.

While the power of naming undoubtedly contributes to the continued focus on women's fear of success and to the neglect of their fears of failure, there is perhaps another less obvious contributant. To fear success does not essentially contradict stereotypic feminine behavior. While success can be defined in a variety of ways, success in a patriarchal culture is, like the generic he, ultimately seen as male. Thus for a woman to fear success is "appropriate" behavior. In contrast, the fear of failure is a contradiction of stereotypic feminine behavior. In a patriarchal culture, not to achieve success, or to fail, is what is expected for women. Thus, a woman who fears failure is feeling (and potentially acting) against the grain of proscribed feminine behavior. The woman who fears success is still acting the way she's supposed to while the woman who fears failure is not. As feminist psychologists we must not ignore this subtle form of (perhaps, but not necessarily, maladaptive) resistance.

REFERENCES

Clance, P. & Imes, S. (1978). The imposter phenomenon in high achieving women: Dynamics and therapeutic intervention. *Psychotherapy: Theory, Research, and Practice*, 15, 241-247.
Henley, N. (1985). Psychology and gender. *Signs: Journal of Women in Culture and Society, 11*, 101-119.

Horner, M. (1968). *Sex differences in achievement motivation and performance in competitive and non-competitive situations.* Unpublished doctoral dissertation, University of Michigan.

Sutherland, E. & Veroff, J. (1985). Achievement motivation and sex roles. In V. O'Leary, R. Unger, and B. Wallston (eds.), *Women, Gender, and Social Psychology* (pp. 101-128). Hillsdale, N.J.: Lawrence Erlbaum Associates.

Tresemer, D. (1977). *Fear of success.* New York: Plenum Press.

The Imposter Phenomenon:
An Internal Barrier
to Empowerment and Achievement

Pauline Rose Clance
Maureen Ann O'Toole

In 1978, Clance and Imes developed the term Impostor Phenomenon (IP) to designate an internal experience of intellectual phoniness which seemed to be particularly prevalent among a select sample of high achieving women. They worked with 150 highly successful women from a wide range of professional fields such as law, nursing, medicine, social work, and university teaching, plus students at graduate and undergraduate levels. Clance and Imes had worked with their subjects in clinical settings such as individual psychotherapy or theme-centered interactional groups or small discussion-oriented college classes. These subjects had obtained earned degrees, high scores on standardized tests, or professional recognition from colleagues or organizations, yet they did not experience an internal sense of success. They were afraid they were "impostors" who did not belong "here with all these bright, competent, people." They were very frightened that others would discover that they were not as competent as they appeared to be, and dreaded such discovery. They attributed their successes to hard work, luck,

Pauline Rose Clance is Professor of Psychology at Georgia State University, Atlanta, GA and is Chair of the Psychotherapy Committee. She is author of *The Imposter Phenomenon: Overcoming the Fear that Haunts Your Success.* For years, she has been Supervisor and Consultant for Kawna, a women's co-op counseling center in Atlanta and has been actively involved in research on women's issues.

Maureen Ann O'Toole is a doctoral candidate in clinical psychology at Georgia State University.

51

knowing the right people, being in the right place at the right time, or to their interpersonal assets such as charm and the ability to relate well, rather than to ability or competence. For instance, students often said the admissions committee had made an error. One student expressed her feelings by saying, "I walk around thinking I'm the Michigan mistake." A highly respected professional woman explained, "I just got my job as a fluke. They needed someone at mid-year and so very few qualified applicants applied." The reality was that the students who were feeling like impostors were among the highest ranked students and the search committee for the woman professional had selected her out of a pool of many highly qualified candidates. These subjects were ingenious at negating objective external evidence that indicated they were indeed very bright. They had tremendous difficulty in accepting compliments or positive feedback. If they received an excellent quarterly evaluation they might think, "This agency or institution does not have very high standards if they think I'm good." Yet, if they received any negative feedback they believed it and tended to remember it as evidence of their deficits.

These women often experienced a terror of failure. They thought if they made a mistake or failed at something, they would feel foolish and be humiliated. Consequently, they went to great lengths to avoid any mistakes or failures.

Clance and Imes indicated that in their clinical work women were primarily the ones who reported this phenomenon, but that whether or not it occurred with men needed to be investigated. All later research that utilized very structured interviews or questionnaires on the Impostor Phenomenon indicates that men do experience the phenomenon with as much frequency as women (Imes, 1979; Harvey, 1981; Lawler, 1984; and Flewelling, 1985). In fact, Topping (1983), in her study of university faculty found the males in her sample were considerably more likely to experience the impostor phenomenon than were the females. Her explanation was that the women may have had to work through more of their IP feelings in order to become faculty members. Although men do not openly acknowledge the Impostor Phenomenon as frequently as women do, when queried in an anonymous and confidential setting they did indicate the presence of these feelings.

The reader may be asking why it matters if a person, man or woman, experiences the IP. Since these feelings do not actually prevent success, why should they be of interest to psychotherapists? The answer to this important question is that self-declared impostors may not be achieving all that they are capable of achieving, and that they are not enjoying their successes. IP sufferers do not have a realistic sense of their own competence and are *not* fully empowered to internalize their strengths, accept their deficits, and function with joy. If impostor feelings are intense, IP sufferers may turn down opportunities to advance. They may simply not attempt to meet their dreams, settling instead for what seems certain. Anxiety, self-doubt, fear of failure, and guilt about success undermine their ability to function at their highest level. They lose the sense of reward and joy that ordinarily accompanies success (Hirschfield, 1982).

So, for women and for men, high levels of IP feelings present a significant problem. The present authors think that IP feelings of an intense or moderate degree (as evidenced by a score above 60 on Clance's IP scale) may prevent more women than men from actually reaching their highest potential. Although men suffer from IP feelings, we believe that women are more likely to be limited, and limited more powerfully, by the Impostor Phenomenon.

The first author of this paper saw many women turn down the invitation to do honors work at a small, private, highly rated college. In fact, at that college from 1969-1973 women were significantly less likely to do honors work than men were, although they entered the college with SAT scores, grades and recommendations as good as those of the men. When this difference between the sexes and the Impostor Phenomenon was discussed with women students in small groups, women began to label their fears as "impostor fears" and to decide to do honors work in spite of them. They dealt with these fears in individual and group therapy, and the next year (1974), the number of women who did honors work increased significantly. Since men were likely experiencing the Impostor Phenomenon at the same frequency, why did it impact women more? The opinion of the present authors is that the men were encouraged by mentors, faculty, and the society to go ahead and do honors in spite of their impostor fears. They were encouraged to override their fears and to go for success.

Imposter fears may interfere more with women's functioning for a number of reasons. In addition to lacking the encouragement and support which are offered to men, women may be further handicapped by an inability to resolve certain dilemmas from childhood. Benjamin (1984) postulates that, although human beings are born with capacities for self-assertion, autonomy, and relatedness, girls feel a conflict between being feminine like mother and yet wanting to be active, autonomous and separate, like father. They are torn between autonomy and femininity and between being a nurturer and being independent. Eichenbaum and Orbach (1982) suggest that because of a mother's own history and lack of fulfillment of her own needs, she acts ambivalently toward the daughter's need for separation and independence. The mother wants to hold the daughter close and may interfere with her moves toward separateness and independence. Instead, she may teach her to negate her own needs and to give to others what she may need herself: nurturing. The daughter learns to feel uncomfortable with her own needs and her own autonomy but quite comfortable in nurturing others. Thus, fundamental child rearing patterns which encourage stereotyped gender roles contribute to women's conflict over autonomy. When a woman experiences IP feelings due to particular family dynamics, her feelings are intensified by these general child rearing patterns which make her conflicted about her autonomy.

Nurturing others is supported by society and much of a woman's socialization is, in fact, training to nurture others. Because they are not as conflicted about nurturing and because society at all levels expects and supports their being nurturing, the women we deal with are more likely to have many more responsibilities than men in similar positions. In addition to their career, work, or academic position, they expect themselves and are expected by society to take on many responsibilities and care for the home and any children, work on their relationships, caretake for parents and family, etc. They are expected to do well at their jobs and to do everything else. It is all right for them to have careers provided they fulfill all of their other duties first. Guilt about the career is a common experience.

Mathilde Krim, the prominent microbiologist, when asked about the status of women in science, replied:

> When I was starting in Switzerland, society generally thought women going into science were forsaking their normal way of life, that they were rare exceptions, a little bizarre. People used to think female scientists were either destined to become spinsters or that they were amateurs, spoiled girls wasting our time. Today it's quite different. Many women going into science believe that they can make a career and still have a family life. Back then I had serious doubts that I could do both. Those doubts still persist. I often think that I am not good at anything I do, that neither my work nor the care of my family is being done properly. I have an almost constant feeling of guilt. Male colleagues don't understand it. (Lawren, 1985)

When these external variables and internal conflicts as described by Benjamin, Orbach and Eichenbaum, and Krim are combined with the Impostor Phenomenon, they create important barriers to women's sense of competence and empowerment, which impact on their level of accomplishment. Further research is needed to check these hypothesized differences between men and women regarding the impact of high Impostor scores.

In addition to the treatment of particular impostor issues, we think that women can, in their work with the therapist, resolve the conflict around the issues of autonomy and relatedness and can affirm both aspects of their being. They also can develop a respect for their own needs and wants, as Eichenbaum and Orbach so vividly describe in their work.

We think it is also necessary to work for societal changes that will encourage and support women's needs to achieve.

DESCRIPTION OF THE IMPOSTER PHENOMENON

This paper is too short to describe all of the features of persons experiencing strong IP beliefs, but the reader can find a thorough description in the articles referenced. Very briefly, some of the features that accompany IP beliefs in the typical female client are listed below.

1. The Imposter Cycle. The person faces an exam or project or task. She experiences great doubt and fear. She questions whether or not she will succeed *this* time. She may experience anxiety, psychosomatic symptoms, nightmares, etc. She works hard and overprepares, or, procrastinates and then prepares in a frenzied manner. She succeeds and receives positive feedback. The whole cycle is reinforced. She may have the superstitious belief, "I must suffer in order to succeed." Doubting is reinforced (Clance & Imes, 1978; Clance, 1985).

2. Introversion. Introverted persons are much more likely to have high IP scores (Lawler, 1984).

3. Dread of Evaluation. She hypothesizes that others will know all that she doesn't know.

4. Terror of Failure. She is very afraid of the shame and humiliation associated with "looking foolish."

5. Guilt About Success. She handles this by denying her success.

6. Great Difficulty in Internalizing Positive Feedback. She has trouble experiencing the excitement that comes with the acceptance of such feedback. She avoids the excitement that would come if she accepted praise. She has difficulty dealing with energy and excitement and is afraid of the effects.

7. Generalized Anxiety.

8. Overestimating Others While Underestimating Oneself. She has a tremendous respect for the intellect of others and a tendency to compare her weaknesses with the strengths of others. Therefore, she undervalues her own abilities and overestimates others' assets.

9. Defining Intelligence in a Skewed Manner. She has many myths about intelligence and what constitutes intelligence, and these usually work to her detriment.

10. False and Non-affirming Family Messages. She has received messages from her family which contradict others'

messages about her competence, and her family has, sub-
tly or overtly, refused to recognize her specific assets
(Clance & Imes, 1978; Grays, 1985).

IMPOSTER PHENOMENON TREATMENT ISSUES

We see the empathic, supportive, nonauthoritarian therapeutic
relationship as the necessary background for dealing with the issues and concerns specific to Impostor Phenomenon sufferers.
All of the following treatment techniques presume this relationship as a context. Within that context, our goals are to assist the
client in moving away from the attitudes and beliefs that have
been at the root of her suffering, and toward an expanded sense
of self which incorporates her formerly disowned creativity, intelligence and capability (Imes & Clance, 1984; Matthews &
Clance, 1985).

Impostor feelings are not customarily part of the client's initial
presentation, so the first task of the therapist in the developing
therapeutic alliance is to identify these feelings as they arise. The
Impostor Phenomenon may manifest initially in many different
ways, the two primary ones being an inordinate amount of anxiety and pain associated with accomplishment in a high-achiever,
or a lack of ambition or accomplishment in an apparently capable
woman. The skilled therapist is alert to material indicating either
of these experiences.

The therapist may notice anxiety about completing tasks, fears
about not doing good work, or immobilization in the face of large
tasks. When faced with a large project, the Impostor Phenomenon sufferer will consistently move away from others, particularly supportive others, acting in such a way as to isolate herself
with her fears. The therapist begins to break down this isolation
by identifying it as a pattern and being with the client as she
experiences the pain of it.

Another behavior that may indicate Impostor Phenomenon issues in a client is rigidity about tasks and goals. When a client
believes that everything she does must conform to an internal
standard of excellence that the therapist cannot distinguish from
perfection, the Impostor Phenomenon must be considered. This

lack of ability to recognize and accept a range of possible performance levels is essentially a cognitive distortion, and the therapist's work in recognizing and labelling it is an important first
step toward change.

Another clue that may alert the therapist to the presence of
underlying Impostor Phenomenon dynamics is a disparity between what the client is apparently capable of and the goals she
sets for herself. If a client is employed in a position for which she
is overeducated, she may be suffering from Impostor feelings. A
woman who consistently believes that she is capable of less than
she appears to be capable of, or less than she has accomplished in
the past, may be crippled by not believing in her capabilities. It is
important for the therapist in the initial stages of therapy to be
alert to this and to reflect what she hears to the client.

A fourth, and more subtle, indicator of Impostor Phenomenon
issues occurs when an apparently capable client focuses exclusively on family or relationship issues and fails to bring up any
achievement-related issues. This omission ought to be investigated to determine whether it is part of a pattern of ignoring or
negating achievement needs because of underlying fears of an
inability to perform successfully.

When a therapist, for these or other reasons, begins to suspect
IP dynamics, she is advised to use the Clance IP scale to test her
hypothesis (Clance, 1985; Edwards, 1983; Holmes, 1985). A cut-
off score of 60 is recommended to identify Impostor sufferers.
The scale itself can serve as a useful therapeutic tool to enable
therapist and client to discuss and label the client's feelings. The
information that what she is experiencing is experienced by others, that it can be named, and that it can be addressed in therapy,
is an affirmation of the client and is often met with a great deal of
relief.

As the therapist becomes aware of the client's Impostor Phenomenon issues, she needs to take the client's fears and doubts
seriously. This is crucial to further progress in therapy. Most
impostors have a long history of being discounted when they
attempt to make contact with others by sharing their real fears
and doubts. This reinforces their long-standing isolation and
leads to an escalation of these painful dynamics. The therapist

must take care not to replicate this experience. A period of exploration, with the therapist obtaining as many specifics as possible about the client's fearful fantasies and anxious self-talk, is in order. As the client shares the exact nature of her thoughts and feelings regarding successful achievement, the therapist functions as an accepting and affirming other in regard to her feelings, while at the same time helping the client to become aware of the thinking distortions involved.

The second area to be examined with IP sufferers is family of origin dynamics and script messages. A detailed and thorough family history is necessary to help the client become aware of the roles assigned in the family and how her role in the family is impacting on her current thoughts and feelings. The typical IP sufferer has received one of two messages from her family: she may have been told that she is not the bright one in the family, or that she is the bright one and that this means that everything she does will come easily and without effort (Clance, 1985; Imes & Clance, 1984).

Our approach combines cognitive restructuring and some Gestalt work in a framework of empathic relating. We find that group therapy is often helpful to help the IP sufferer begin to see herself in a more realistic way. As she meets other obviously bright and capable people who do not easily accept positive feedback and do not own their competence, she is moved to recognize the unreasonableness of her view of herself.

Techniques we have found helpful include having the client fantasize aspects of the problem and some solutions. We may have her fantasize conversations with significant persons whom she believes she has fooled about her competence. We may have her fantasize feeling successful and sharing her successes with family members, sometimes in a bragging manner. We may have her fantasize not doing something perfectly. All of these fantasies can generate material for examination of the underlying dynamics that contribute to the clients' suffering.

We have asked some women to keep a journal to become aware of such things as positive feedback they receive and discount, times they do or say things they don't want to in order to gain approval, and ways they stop themselves from taking risks or revealing themselves to others. We sometimes help the client examine upcoming projects and make clear decisions about her level of investment, how much time she will put in, and what degree of "imperfection" she will accept in herself and her work.

In these ways, we work with the client's cognitive processes as well as her emotions. As we address the cognitive distortions revealed through the journal process, strong emotions surface. We expect to find fear, guilt, buried resentments, and shame. This shame is often rooted in the client's socialization for femininity, which has taught her to value any ability she has to nurture and to be ashamed of her ambition and achievement needs. Resistances to the therapeutic process may indicate the need to deal with this shame, which the IP sufferer has kept at bay by ambivalently being successful but not enjoying it. She may fear that in uncovering her shame she will be disrupting the delicate balance of her ambivalence, and lose her ability to achieve. Or, she may fear that if she allows herself to remove the restraints placed upon her by that shame, she will become a ruthless monster of overwhelming ambition. Such a spectre is not infrequently called upon as a warning to women: the hard-driving career woman who is not "feminine," has no close relationships, and ends up alone.

The therapeutic process with IP sufferers is often slow and requires a great deal of patience. However, we have found it to be richly rewarding. IP sufferers are very capable people, and when they begin to focus on changing themselves, they are very impactful, as they are in other areas of their lives.

THE IMPOSTER PHENOMENON*

It is best to give the first response that enters your mind rather than dwelling on each statement and thinking about it over and over.

1. I have often succeeded on a test or task even though I was afraid that I would not do well before I undertook the task.

1	2	3	4	5
(not at all true)	(rarely)	(sometimes)	(often)	(very true)

2. I can give the impression that I'm more competent than I really am.

1	2	3	4	5

3. I avoid evaluations if possible and have a dread of others evaluating me.

1	2	3	4	5

4. When people praise me for something I've accomplished, I'm afraid I won't be able to live up to their expectations of me in the future.

1	2	3	4	5

5. I sometimes think I obtained my present position or gained my present success because I happened to be in the right place at the right time or knew the right people.

1	2	3	4	5

6. I'm afraid people important to me may find out that I'm not as capable as they think I am.

1	2	3	4	5

7. I tend to remember the incidents in which I have not done my best more than those times I have done my best.

1	2	3	4	5

8. I rarely do a project or task as well as I'd like to do it.

1	2	3	4	5

9. Sometimes I feel or believe that my success in my life or in my job has been the result of some kind of error.

1	2	3	4	5

10. It's hard for me to accept compliments or praise about my intelligence or accomplishments.

    1   2   3   4   5

11. At times, I feel my success was due to some kind of luck.

    1   2   3   4   5

12. I'm disappointed at times in my present accomplishments and think I should have accomplished much more.

    1   2   3   4   5

13. Sometimes I'm afraid others will discover how much knowledge or ability I really lack.

    1   2   3   4   5

14. I'm often afraid that I may fail at a new assignment or undertaking even though I generally do well at what I attempt.

    1   2   3   4   5

15. When I've succeeded at something and received recognition for my accomplishments, I have doubts that I can keep repeating that success.

    1   2   3   4   5

16. If I receive a great deal of praise and recognition for something I've accomplished, I tend to discount the importance of what I have done.

    1   2   3   4   5

17. I often compare my ability to those around me and think they may be more intelligent than I am.

    1   2   3   4   5

18. I often worry about not succeeding with a project or on an examination, even though others around me have considerable confidence that I will do well.

    1   2   3   4   5

19. If I'm going to receive a promotion or gain recognition of some kind, I hesitate to tell others until it is an accomplished fact.

   1   2   3   4   5

20. I feel bad and discouraged if I'm not "the best" or at least "very special" in situations that involve achievement.

   1   2   3   4   5

REFERENCES

Benjamin, J. (1984). The convergence of psychoanalysis and feminism: Gender identity and autonomy. In C. Brody (Ed.), *Women Therapists Working with Women: New Theory and Process of Feminist Therapy*. New York: Springer Publishing.

Clance, P.R. (1985). *The Impostor Phenomenon: Overcoming the Fear that Haunts Your Success*. Atlanta: Peachtree Publishers.

Clance, P.R. & Imes, S.A. (1978). The Impostor Phenomenon in high achieving women: Dynamics and therapeutic intervention. *Psychotherapy: Theory, Research and Practice, 15*(3), 241-247.

Edwards, P.W. (1983). *A validation study of the Impostor Phenomenon Scale*. Unpublished manuscript. University of Georgia, Department of Psychology, Athens.

Eichenbaum, L. & Orbach, S. (1984). Feminist psychoanalysis: Theory and practice. In C. Brody (Ed.), *Women Therapists Working with Women: New Theory and Process of Feminist Therapy*. New York: Springer Publishing.

Flewelling, A.L. (1985). *The Impostor Phenomenon in individuals succeeding in self-perceived atypical professions: The effects of mentoring and longevity*. Unpublished master's thesis, Georgia State University, Atlanta.

Grays, L.A. (1985). *The relation between the Impostor Phenomenon and atypicality of race, educational attainment, socioeconomic status, and career in college women*. Unpublished master's thesis, Georgia State University, Atlanta.

Harvey, J.C. (1981). The Impostor Phenomenon and achievement: A failure to internalize success (Doctoral Dissertation, Temple University, 1981). *Dissertation Abstracts International, 42*, 4969A.

Hirschfield, M.M. (1982). The Impostor Phenomenon in successful career women (Doctoral Dissertation, Fordham University, 1982). *Dissertation Abstracts International, 43*, 1722B.

Holmes, S.W. (1985). *The Impostor Phenomenon: A validity study of Clance's IP scale*. Unpublished master's thesis, Georgia State University, Atlanta.

Imes, S.A. (1979). The Impostor Phenomenon as a function of attribution patterns and internalized masculinity/femininity in high achieving women and men (Doctoral Dissertation, Georgia State University, 1979). *Dissertation Abstracts International, 40*, 5868B-5869B.

Imes, S.A. & Clance, P.R. (1984). Treatment of the Impostor Phenomenon in high achieving women. In C. Brody (Ed.), *Women Therapists Working with Women: New Theory and Process of Feminist Therapy*. New York: Springer Publishing.

Lawler, N.K. (1984). The Impostor Phenomenon in high achieving persons and Jungian personality variables (Doctoral Dissertation, Georgia State University, 1984). *Dissertation Abstracts International, 45*, 86.

Lawren, B. (1985). Interview: Mathilde Krim, *Omni, 8*: 76-78. New York: Omni Publications.

Matthews, A. & Clance, P.R. (1985). Treatment of the Impostor Phenomenon in Psychotherapy Clients. *Psychotherapy in Private Practice, 3*(1), 71-81.

Topping, M.E.H. (1983). The Impostor Phenomenon: A study of its construct and incidence in university faculty members (Doctoral Dissertation, University of South Florida, 1983). *Dissertation Abstracts International, 41*, 4248A-4249A.

Career Aspiration
in Black College Women:
An Examination of Performance
and Social Self-Esteem

Cheryl R. Bailey
Martha T. Mednick

Despite the increasing entry of women into the labor force and consequent interest in the social psychological foundation of career aspirations, gaps abound in the literature. One major inadequacy is the approach to the measurement of women's career aspirations. For example, occupations usually defined as nontraditional may have sub-specialties or other characteristics that do conform to the demands and characteristics of women's traditional role and may be viewed as traditional by the aspirant. This suggests information concerning the individual's image of her future field, in addition to statements about career goals, is needed. Another problematic area concerns the question of how self-esteem should be defined and measured when attempting to predict career goals. Global scales have been poor predictors of women's achievement behavior, but specific scales have been found to be more efficacious (Deaux, 1976).

Cheryl R. Bailey is Chief of Research of the Washington, DC Superior Court Social Services Division. Her research interests are in the area of black women's career aspirations.

Martha T. Mednick is Professor of Psychology at Howard University. She has written extensively on women and achievement.

This article is based in part on a doctoral dissertation submitted to Howard University by the senior author. Requests for reprints should be sent to Cheryl Bailey, 1724 Shilling Lane, Silver Spring, MD 20906.

Data on black women were used as the frame of reference, for both career aspiration measures.

65

The current study takes a new approach by utilizing a multi-dimensional approach to the examination of self-esteem and career aspirations. In particular, we examine the relationship between performance/ability, social self-esteem, and career aspiration among a group that has been relatively neglected, black women (Murray & Mednick, 1977; Smith, 1982). It should be noted that we are not interested in race or sex comparisons, but rather are taking a look at variations among black women.

Empirical research on self-esteem has usually employed global self-evaluative measures (Rosenberg, 1965; Wylie, 1974, 1979) and has thus assumed that self-evaluations are stable, unidimensional, and remain constant across dimensions of self and situations. However, this global conceptualization of self-esteem has been criticized (Frank & Marolla, 1976; Simpson & Boyle, 1975). In particular, Simpson and Boyle (1975) assert that global self-esteem measures are too general to permit specific behavioral predictions. Self-esteem as a multidimensional construct has been supported by several factor analytic studies (Berger, 1968; Norem-Hebeisen, 1976). Others have noted that some of the contradictory findings about women's self-esteem may be attributed to the conceptualization of self-esteem as a unidimensional, rather than as a multidimensional trait (O'Brien, 1980; Stake & Orlofsky, 1981; Wylie, 1979)

In order to examine this possibility, and to look more closely at women's self-confidence about achievement, Stake (1979) developed a scale that taps self-evaluation of ability/performance, the Performance Self-Esteem Scale (PSES). It also includes items that measure social self-esteem. She found that, in contrast to global self-esteem, male undergraduates scored significantly higher than female undergraduates on the PSES (Stake, 1979). Most germane to our study was the finding that high PSES was related to strength of career commitment and involvement for women business school undergraduates.

Black women's career aspirations and achievement behavior have been studied only indirectly in relation to self-esteem. Mednick and Murray (1975) found that black women with high achievement motivation attributed their successes more to ability than those with low achievement motivation. Such an attributional pattern may imply positive attitudes about achievement and thus higher PSES for these women, the hypothesis that we pursue in this study.

Turning to the problematic nature of the measurement of traditionality of women's aspirations, investigators typically use a statistical definition which defines traditionality in terms of the percentage of women (or men) in the field. Examples of statistically traditional female occupations are elementary school teachers, health workers and clerical workers. Conversely, nontraditional work is in fields in which women form a considerably smaller proportion of the workforce than their share in the total population of employees (e.g., physicians, architects, dentists, and engineers) (Cahn, 1979). An alternate method of defining traditionality of careers is to measure perceived traditionality (Chunn, 1976; Thomas, 1983). Here the individual is asked for a subjective rating of the traditionality of her choice. Thomas (1983) found that traditionality thus defined was related to fear of success and delay of gratification.

A specific subjective factor that may enter into women's career choices may be their reasons for selecting a chosen field. For example, Mednick (1981) found that women who had chosen the statistically nontraditional field of pharmacy said they did so because it was an occupation whose structure, such as availability of part-time work possibilities, and of work close to home, could allow coordination of work and family life. Thus, the reason for the pursuit was traditional, that is, it is an explanation that is compatible with female sex role expectations. Such an explanation of the choice casts career classification in a somewhat different light, and suggests that a combination of the statistical and the subjective may provide a more analytical way of measuring choice than either of the two definitions taken alone. In this study we construct two typologies, one combines statistical traditionality with reasons given for entering the career, the second does the same with perceived traditionality, the subjective measure.

We thus argue that women who aspire to nontraditional careers are not a homogeneous group, and that women who plan to enter nontraditional fields for nontraditional reasons (e.g., to exercise leadership) may be more similar to women aspiring to traditional fields for nontraditional reasons than to other nontraditional women. In this study we examined PSES and social self-esteem as related to the multidimensional measures of career choice.

METHOD

Subject

The subjects were 250 black junior and senior women from Howard University who were paid for their voluntary participation. Junior and senior women were used because career decisions are most likely to be salient during this period (Parsons, Frieze & Ruble, 1978).

Instruments

Self-esteem was assessed with Stake's (1979) Performance Self-Esteem Scale (PSES). The PSES is composed of 47 items which are related to performance in achievement settings and which tap social self-esteem. Forty items measure performance self-esteem and seven items tap social self-esteem. Subjects indicated on a 7 point Likert Scale the extent to which each item described them.

An objective, as well as a subjective measure, was used to tap career aspiration. In addition to questions about career goals, the subject's perception of the traditionality of her career choice was measured by an occupational choice questionnaire which included a two-item revised form of the Chunn-Thomas Perceived Traditionality Career Choice Scale. Subjects were asked the following questions: "When you think of the career you are planning to pursue, how traditional or non-traditional do you feel it is for women in general?" and "Please rate your career as its being traditional or nontraditional for black women." The questionnaire also included items adapted from Tangri's (1969) measure in which individuals were asked to rate the degree of importance of a number of factors for their career decision. Several of the factors examined were: advancement, leadership and responsibility, chance to work with people, and allows me to run a household. The factors were scored as "other" or "self" oriented, for use in the typology.

Procedure

The data were collected in two sessions. In session one, each subject was given a booklet which contained the instruments. Several measures not relevant to the present study were gathered at the same time (see Bailey, 1982). During the second session, each subject was interviewed by a female confederate who posed as a younger student desiring information on how to choose a career. The questions asked during the second session focused on the process by which subjects arrived at their particular career goals and their career commitment (Mednick, 1981; Tangri, 1969). Several items in the interview served as reliability checks on similar items in the self-administered questionnaire. At the close of the second session each subject was thoroughly debriefed.

RESULTS

A fourfold classification scheme contrasting the traditionality of the career choice with the reasons given for entering a field was used to create a typology. The subjects were classified as traditional-congruent, traditional-noncongruent, nontraditional-congruent and nontraditional-noncongruent types, using both the statistical (U.S. Department of Labor, 1980), and the perceived measures of traditionality. A type is congruent when the level of traditionality of the career choice and the reasons given for entering it are similar. For example, a woman aspiring to a traditional field (e.g., nursing) who explains her choice in other-oriented terms (e.g., to help others) would be a traditional-congruent type. On the other hand, when a type is noncongruent, the traditionality of the career choice and the reasons given for entering it differ. For example, aspiration to a traditional career (e.g., nursing) explained in self-oriented terms (e.g., to exercise leadership) would be referred to as a traditional-noncongruent type.

Table 1 shows that almost half of the women sampled fell in the nontraditional-noncongruent group. The statistical traditionality typology was similar, with about 35% of the women falling into the nontraditional-noncongruent group. That is, most of the women aspiring to careers in nontraditional areas were giving

Table 1

Frequency Tables for the Career Aspiration Typologies

a. Perceived Traditionality Congruence Typology for Black Women:

Congruence	Perceived Traditionality		Total
	Traditional	Nontraditional	
Noncongruent	21	116	137
Congruent	37	67	104
Total	58	183	241

b. Statistical Traditionality Congruence Typology for Black Women:

Congruence	Statistical Traditionality		Total
	Traditional	Nontraditional	
Noncongruent	25	86	111
Congruent	70	63	133
Total	95	149	244

traditional explanations. The most typical reason give for the career choice was "to help others," and this was true for both the objective and subjective career aspiration measures.

Perceived Traditionality and Self-Esteem

The results of the one-way analysis of variance for the performance/ability dimension of self-esteem revealed significant differences among the perceived traditionality career aspiration groups ($F = 4.22$; $d.f. = 3,227$; $p = .006$). Examination of the results of the paired comparisons, using Scheffés test, indicated that the overall effect of performance/ability self-esteem was due to subjects in the perceived nontraditional-congruent group reporting higher self-estimates of performance and ability than subjects in the perceived nontraditional-noncongruent group (Table 2).

In contrast to this finding, the results of the analysis of variance of social self-esteem scores revealed no significant differences ($F = 1.16$; d.f. $= 237$; n.s.).

Statistical Traditionality Congruence Typology and Self-Esteem

When the analysis focused on the objective measure of traditionality and performance/ability self-esteem, the one-way analysis of variance was also found to be significant ($F = 4.71$; $d.f. = 3,240$, $p = .003$). Table 3 shows that the statistical nontraditional-congruent group was significantly different from the statistical traditional-congruent group, with the nontraditional-congruent group reporting higher self-evaluations of ability and performance. In addition, there was a tendency for the traditional-noncongruent group to report a higher level of ability/performance self-esteem than subjects in the traditional-congruent group. Subjects in the statistical traditional-congruent group reported the lowest level of performance/ability self-esteem of all the statistical career aspiration groups.

As with the subjective measure of career aspiration, the four objective career aspiration groups did not differ significantly on the social self-esteem dimension.

DISCUSSION

Most studies have viewed career aspiration in unidimensional terms and have assumed that women aspiring to traditional fields are traditional in other respects. However, the stereotypic conception of the woman in a female dominated career as one who devalues the development of achievement goals in order to fulfill

Table 2

Results of One-Way Analysis of Variance and Paired Comparisons for Performance and Social
Self-Esteem as a Function of Perceived Traditionality Congruence Typology for Black Women

| Self-Esteem Dimension | Perceived Traditionality Career Aspiration Group | | | | F-value One-way ANOVA |
	Traditional Congruent	Traditional Noncongruent	Nontraditional Noncongruent	Nontraditional Congruent	
Performance/Ability Self-Esteem	$\bar{x}$=89.32 S.D.=17.39	$\bar{x}$=96.62 S.D.=22.04	$\bar{x}$=87.15[a] S.D.=16.33	$\bar{x}$=95.42[a] S.D.=17.02	4.22 *
Social Self-Esteem	$\bar{x}$=42.59 S.D.=5.83	$\bar{x}$=44.00 S.D.=5.34	$\bar{x}$=41.87 S.D.=5.07	$\bar{x}$=41.75 S.D.=5.49	1.16

* $p < .01$

Note A common subscript (a) identifies group means differing significantly at $p < .10$ using
Scheffé's test.

Table 3

Results of One-Way Analysis of Variance and Paired Comparisons for Performance and Social Self-Esteem as a Function of Statistical Traditionality Congruence Typology for Black Women

Self-Esteem Dimension	Statistical Traditionality Career Aspiration Group				F-value One-way ANOVA
	Traditional-Congruent	Traditional-Noncongruent	Nontraditional-Noncongruent	Nontraditional-Congruent	
Performance/Ability Self-Esteem	$\bar{x}$=85.76 [ab] S.D.=17.33	$\bar{x}$=97.56 [b] S.D.=19.36	$\bar{x}$=89.48 S.D.=15.82	$\bar{x}$=94.97 [a] S.D.=17.85	4.71 *
Social Self-Esteem	$\bar{x}$=42.61 S.D.=4.70	$\bar{x}$=43.60 S.D.=4.48	$\bar{x}$=41.53 S.D.=5.62	$\bar{x}$=41.76 S.D.=5.82	1.29

*$p < .01$

Note   Common subscripts (a,b) identify group means differing significantly at $p < .10$ using Scheffé's test.

73

the demands of the female role, such as attending to the needs of others, was not supported in the present investigation. Similarly, support was not found for the view that women aspiring to non-traditional careers necessarily value achievement goals, while forsaking interpersonal concerns.

Interestingly, women who stated they entered their field for self-oriented (nontraditional) reasons reported higher self-esti-mates of performance and ability in achievement settings, than those who entered their fields for other-oriented reasons (tradi-tional), regardless of the traditionality of the career choice. That is, women aspiring to traditional and nontraditional careers who entered their field for "nontraditional" reasons reported the highest self-estimates of ability and performance in achievement settings. The findings also confirm Stake's (1979) findings that self-esteem is multidimensional.

We believe that this study suggests an important refinement in the study of women's career aspirations, one that moves us away from stereotypes about the women or the field, and certainly from any categorical ideas about women's fear of success, im-postor syndromes, or self-sabotaging behavior. The findings about self-esteem fly in the face of these widely shared beliefs. The reasons for a woman's aspirations and commitments are as important as the gender composition of the field, and tell us a great deal about how to avoid such stereotypes.

Finally, this study is about black women and adds to our knowledge about this neglected group, also victims of stereo-types, albeit of another sort. It is probably the case that these findings would generalize to the majority population, hypotheses worth further exploration.

REFERENCES

Bailey, C. R. (1982). *Career aspiration and commitment in Black college women: An examination of background, attitudinal cognitive factors.* Unpublished doctoral dis-sertation. Howard University, Washington, DC

Berger, C. (1968). Sex differences related to the self-esteem factor structure. *Journal of Consulting and Clinical Psychology, 32,* 442-446.

Cahn, A. (Ed.) (1976). *Women in the U.S. labor force.* New York: Praeger.

Chun, E. (1976). *Black females' choices of traditional and nontraditional careers as related to personal sex-role ideology, perception of significant males' sex-role ideology and perceived socioeconomic status.* Unpublished master's thesis, Howard University, Washington, DC

Deaux, K. (1976). *The behavior of men and women.* Monterey, California: Brooks/ Cole.

Frank, D. & Marolla, J. (1976). Efficacious action and social approval as interacting dimensions of self-esteem: Alternative formulation through construct validation. *Sociometry, 39*, 324-341.

Gecas, V. (1971). Parental behavior and dimensions of adolescent self-evaluation. *Sociometry, 34*, 466-482.

Mednick, M. (1981). Factors influencing role innovative career striving in black and white college women: The effect of expectancies, causal attribution, sex-role concept and achievement related motives. *Catalog of Selected Documents in Psychology.*

Murray, S. R. & Mednick, M. T. (1975). Perceiving the causes of success and failure in achievement: Sex, race and motivational comparisons. *Journal of Consulting and Clinical Psychology, 43*, 881-885.

Murray, S. R. & Mednick, M. T. (1977). Black women's achievement orientation: Motivation and cognitive factors. *Psychology of Women Quarterly, 1*, 274-259.

Norem-Hebeisen, A. (1976). A multidimensional construct of self-esteem. *Journal of Educational Psychology, 68*, 559-565.

O'Brien, E. (1980). The self-report inventory: Development and validation of a multidimensional measure of the self-concept and sources of self-esteem. Unpublished doctoral dissertation, University of Massachusetts.

Parsons, J., Frieze, I. & Ruble, I. (1978). Intrapsychic factors influencing career aspirations in college women. *Sex Roles, 4*, 337-347.

Rosenberg, M. (1965). *Society and the adolescent self-image.* Princeton, NJ: Princeton University Press.

Simpson, C. & Boyle, D. (1975). Esteem construct generality and academic performance. *Educational and Psychological Measurement, 35*, 897-904.

Smith, E.J. (1982). The black female adolescent: A review of the educational, career and psychological literature. *Psychology of Women Quarterly, 6*(3), 261-288.

Stake, J. (1979). The ability/performance dimension of self-esteem. Implications for women's achievement behavior. *Psychology of Women Quarterly, 3*, 365-377.

Stake, J. & Orlofsky, J. (1981). On the use of global and specific measures in assessing the self-esteem of males and females. *Sex Roles: A Journal of Research, 7*, 653-662.

Tangri, S. (1969). *Role innovation in occupational choice among college women.* Unpublished doctoral dissertation, University of Michigan.

Thomas, V. (1983). Perceived traditionality and non-traditionality of career aspirations of black college women. *Perceptual and Motor Skills, 57*, 979-982.

U.S. Department of Labor, Bureau of Labor Statistics. (1980). *Household data annual averages.* Washington, DC: U.S. Government Printing Office.

Wylie, R. (1974). *The self-concept: A review of methodological considerations and measuring instruments.* (vol. 1, rev. ed.) Lincoln: University of Nebraska.

Wylie, R. (1979). *The self-concept: Theory and research on selected topics.* (Vol. 2, rev. ed.), Lincoln: Nebraska Press.

The Phenomenon of Worry: Theory, Research, Treatment and Its Implications for Women

Janet M. Stavosky
Thomas D. Borkovec

Worry is an increasingly widespread phenomenon in our society (Vernoff, Douvan & Kulka, 1981). We have all experienced worry, and it is reported often in clinical interactions and in the description of a variety of psychological complaints. However, despite the pervasiveness of this phenomenon, worry has been essentially ignored in the literature. Our research group has begun to examine the process of worry and the characteristics of the chronic worrier. Several findings are particularly relevant for the present discussion — worry is highly correlated with measures of anxiety and fear, and the majority of self-reported worriers are women. As such, this paper reviews worry research, theory, and treatment, and discusses implications of this area for women.

EARLY RESEARCH

Our interest in worry was initiated by certain findings in insomnia research (cf. Borkovec, 1979) and stimulated by our personal experience and our clients' symptomatic reports. Insomniacs frequently complain of negative, cognitive intrusions when attempting to fall asleep. Reducing these intrusions through re-

Janet M. Stavosky is currently an intern at the Long Beach VA Medical Center completing her doctoral training with Pennsylvania State University. She works primarily in the areas of worry, health psychology, and the psychology of women.

Thomas D. Borkovec is a professor of psychology at Pennsylvania State University conducting research in anxiety disorders and worry.

77

laxation appears to be one of the most effective ways of improving sleep. Therefore, these negative cognitive intrusions, what we describe as "worry," seem to play an important role in the maintenance and treatment of insomnia.

As we explored the literature, we realized that worry plays a role not only in insomnia but also in a variety of other clinical problems. Intrusive, negative thoughts and self-statements are symptomatic of depression and a variety of anxiety disorders (Beck, 1976; Dow & Craighead, 1982). DSM-III describes uncontrollable, negative ruminations as an important diagnostic criterion for many maladjustments, particularly obsessive-compulsive disorders. However, even with these indications the only previous efforts to examine worry exist in the test-anxiety literature (cf. Deffenbacher, 1980, for a review). Liebert and Morris (1976) reported two major and replicable components of test-anxiety: worry and emotionality. They defined worry as the cognitive component — a focus on negative performance and self-evaluation and a concern about failure. Emotionality refers to the more affective and physiological aspects of test-anxiety. Deffenbacher (1980) indicated that worry appears to be the more important and problematic variable as it interferes with performance.

Our research group became intrigued with this apparently important and widespread phenomenon that no one was examining. We began discussing worry, drawing on personal and clinical experience and the limited relevant literature. We then based our investigations on several preliminary hypotheses and impressions. Worry is a series of negative thoughts and images that intrude into awareness in an uncontrolled manner. Worry involves current life concerns. It is compelling, yet troublesome, recurring throughout the day, without providing solutions to the concerns pondered. Described in this manner, worry represents the cognitive component of anxiety, as suggested in the test-anxiety literature.

Our early research attempted to understand the worry process and to characterize the self-described "worrier." Borkovec, Robinson, Pruzinsky and DePree (1983) found that worry tends to be about the future rather than the past or the present. Worry has a negative, anxious emotional tone that is reflected in worry content and the mood of chronic worriers. Worry is intrusive: it is difficult to shut off and distracts attention from the task at hand. In general, worry was found to correlate highly with measures of anxiety, depression, and fear.

The strongest relationship exists between worry and fear. The worry process results in emotional and physical reactions quite similar to those of fear although somewhat milder in intensity. Worry content is full of fears such as feeling self-conscious, making mistakes, and being criticized. In fact, the greatest concern for the worrier appears to be fear of social-evaluative situations.

These early results provided direction for further research. As we were aware that worry resembles fear, we examined the well-established paradigms that exist for fear. Eysenck (1979) found that fear can incubate, meaning that fear and arousal increase after brief or incomplete exposures to a feared stimulus. Alternately, complete or prolonged exposure produces extinction, or a decrease in fear. Borkovec et al. (1983) found that worriers generally experienced more negative, cognitive intrusions than non-worriers during a monotonous task. However, for both worriers and non-worriers, a 15-minute period of worry increased these intrusions in a subsequent task whereas a quiet relaxation period or a 30-minute worry period did not. This showed that the worry process can incubate. Additionally, we found that once worry was induced it had the same effect on chronic worriers and non-worriers. Differences between worriers and non-worriers are most apparent when they are not particularly worried.

Another fear paradigm helped further our understanding of worry. Mowrer's two stage model of fear suggests that avoidance is crucial in maintaining fear (Mowrer, 1947). In the first stage we learn to avoid cues associated with fear-provoking stimuli. In the second stage, we learn to continue the avoidant behavior as it keeps us from encountering our fear. Perhaps worry functions in a similar manner. Worry does not typically involve well-developed problem-solving; instead it's a review of all potentially fearful alternatives. Worry may be a review of scenarios to be avoided: it may function as a cognitive avoidance of some basic fears.

In early studies, worriers reported that they realize their worries are illogical and an ineffective means of coping. However, they feel that if they do not worry the feared event is somehow more probable. Therefore, not worrying is more anxiety-provoking than worrying. McCarthy and Borkovec (1983) found support for this notion. For both worriers and non-worriers, arousal decreased dramatically during a worry period, and then rose when subjects were asked to focus their attention on their breathing. The worry process may thus serve as a reinforcing, anxiety-reducing, cognitive avoidance of feared material.

Engaging in the worry process may help us avoid fearful situations, but it also seems to have a negative effect on our emotional state and attentional abilities. As in other studies, Pruzinsky (1983) and McCarthy and Borkovec (1983) found that worriers generally experience more cognitive intrusions and distractions during tasks than non-worriers. However, they also found that the worriers' cognitive process was more continuous and contained more negative content. This continuous negative process may explain why worriers often report a more dysphoric mood. Additionally, these studies suggested that for chronic worriers, the worry process occurs frequently throughout the day even without obvious threatening or worrisome cues. What effect might these negative cognitions and affective states have on other processes? The test-anxiety literature again provides some suggestions.

Deffenbacher (1980) concluded that the worry component of test-anxiety consistently interferes with task performance. Worry increases as the potential for social evaluation or failure increases (Morris & Fulmer, 1976). This produces interference, because as worry increases, attention is distracted from the task and focused instead on self-evaluative cognitions (Mandler & Watson, 1966; Neale & Katahn, 1968).

These findings were examined in recent research on the general worry phenomenon. Worriers and non-worriers showed similar performances on simple decision-making tasks (Metzger, Miller, Sofka, Cohen, DiMareno, Bigley & Pennock, 1983). On a more complex categorization task, however, worriers took longer to make decisions when the stimuli were ambiguous. As the choice became unclear and it was possible to fail, worriers' indecisiveness increased. Non-worriers showed no changes in their decision-making. If worry was induced by a 15-minute worry incubation period all subjects demonstrated the same inde-cisiveness. This strongly suggests that it is the worry process that is interfering with performance.

In summary, worry is an intrusive, negative cognitive habit. It is the cognitive component of anxiety, elicited by fearful thoughts or environmental events. The worry process interferes with daily functioning as it increases dysphoria and maintains core fears through cognitive avoidance. Additionally, worry in-hibits performance by drawing attention to self-evaluative rumi-nations and away from the task at hand.

CHARACTERISTICS OF THE WORRIER

In our research, we have defined worriers to be those who report worrying fifty percent or more of each day and feel it is problematic for them. These individuals experience worry as an ongoing trait process. Non-worriers are those who report worry-ing twenty percent or less of each day and do not find worry to be a problem. These individuals experience worry as an intermit-tent, transient state.

Few differences distinguish chronic worriers from non-worri-ers. Surprisingly, the differences that do exist are only apparent when individuals are not particularly worried. If worry is in-duced, as in the incubation studies reported earlier, the worry process and its effects appear to be similar for everyone.

Chronic worriers do experience a generally more dysphoric and hostile mood, increased depression, and elevated trait and state anxiety (Borkovec et al., 1983). Additionally, worriers have more difficulty focusing their attention and take longer to make decisions when faced with ambiguity (Metzger et al., 1983). As incubation of the worry process eliminates most of these differences, it seems likely that the observed variations in affect and performance are due to the more frequent, ongoing worry process of the self-described worrier.

A variety of investigations have examined the characteristics of the chronic worrier. However, an important variable has often been overlooked or ignored: there exists almost no exploration of the fact that most self-reported worriers are female.

GENDER DIFFERENCE IN THE REPORT OF WORRY

In describing one of the earliest studies, Borkovec et al. (1983) reported that worry status was not proportional by gender — women outnumbered men. While screening for relaxation research, Johnson (1981) found that 40% of the females reported being worriers (by our operational definition), as compared to 16% of the males. In a study examining the incubation effects of worry, Borkovec et al. (1983) noted that 88% of their subjects were female. In two studies examining stimulus control treatments of worry, Borkovec, Wilkinson, Folensbee, and Lerman (1983) found that 80% of their high worry subjects were female. Finally, in the general group screening for research subjects it has been repeatedly observed that women report being worriers at a rate two to three times that of men. It would seem that strong indications of a gender difference exist in the report and/or the experience of worry.

Although the data strongly suggest that males and females differ in their report (and perhaps their experience) of worry, none of the research thus far has addressed this phenomenon. Few studies analyzed for gender differences, although some attempted to control for gender effects by having males and females represented proportionally across conditions. It is clear that the examination of apparent gender differences is crucial in any attempt to understand the etiology and process of worry, and the characteristics of the worrier.

To understand these potential differences it is first necessary to clarify the term "gender differences." As Sherif (1982) pointed out, there are many psychological terms that refer to various constructs and concepts regarding gender. Frequently, "gender differences" is used to refer to psychosocial effects, while "sex differences" is reserved for biological or physiological distinctions (Unger, 1979). Although it is impossible to unequivocally define differences as wholly psychosocial or biological, "gender difference" will be used throughout this discussion in reference to the observed psychological differences in worry for males and females.

What might gender differences mean? In the clinical literature, women report more psychological difficulties and are diagnosed as having disturbances more frequently than men (Gove, 1980; Verbrugge, 1980). Females also report higher rates of various disorders including anxieties and phobias (Chambless & Gold-stein, 1980), depression (Weissman, 1980), and hysterical traits (Walowitz, 1972). However, various authors have suggested that what is reflected in these gender differences is not a difference between the sexes, but rather the psychosocial differences in their gender-role identification. This notion is particularly in-triguing in light of recent depression research. Gender differ-ences in adult depression are a consistent and reliable finding. However, Green (1980) found that in adolescents significant group differences existed for gender-role orientation but not gen-der. A feminine or undifferentiated gender-role identification was associated with depression regardless of gender. Current preliminary research in gender differences in worry shows strong tendencies in the same direction (Stavosky, 1986).

As Johnson (1980) emphasized, gender differences should be explored but not for the purpose of demonstrating that one gender has more psychological disturbances than the other. Rather, ex-amining the relationship of gender, gender-roles, and emotional concerns can help clarify what occurs in the constitution and ex-periences of men and women and leads them in different prob-lematic directions (Dohrenwend & Dohrenwend, 1976).

The gender difference in reported worrying may be influenced by two factors. First, women may learn to be more aware of internal states and may more freely disclose such information. Secondly, women may experience worry more frequently and to a greater degree. The contribution of these factors is explored as we discuss the possible theoretical origins of worry and the status of women in our society.

ETIOLOGY OF WORRY

We have some understanding of the experience of worry, the characteristics of the worrier, and how worry may interfere with other activities. But why do people worry? How does worry de-velop and how does it maintain? Finally, what are the constraints that lead women to worry (or report worry) more than men? To

explore these questions we first discuss relevant models of fear
and anxiety.

Worry as Fear

As we have discussed, the experience of worry is closely associated with the process of fear. Of course, fear is an adaptive
response to real environmental threats, resulting in a behavioral
"flight or fight" response. The worry sequence can also be initiated by a feared cue, and results in a cognitive process or response. However, the worrisome stimulus can spring from
within, as a fearful thought or image. Our research indicates that
the situations of most concern to the worrier are social-evaluative
in nature. Our experience and various findings lead us to suggest
that the underlying concern for the worrier is a fear of failure or
rejection.

Fear can result in behavioral avoidance. Analagously, worry
can be conceptualized as cognitive avoidance. People may engage in worry about any number of topics because it helps them
to avoid confrontation with their underlying fear. The content of
the current worry may be only distantly related to this real fear,
hypothetically the fear of negative societal and self-perception.

If this is the case, then to avoid failure and rejection, mistakes
must be avoided by either anticipating all possible negative outcomes or avoiding decisions that may result in censure or negative feedback. Accordingly, we find that worriers are preoccu-
pied with how they are perceived, they review all potential
situations, and they become indecisive when a choice could
mean potential failure or rejection.

Cognitive Avoidance

Worry is seen as the cognitive component of anxiety. When
we discussed worry and fear, we suggested that one role of worry
is to cognitively avoid core fears. Let us now examine cognitive
avoidance and its role in anxiety.

We encounter a stimulus and our primary reaction is to determine whether it is good or bad, and therefore whether it should
be approached or avoided. We judge the stimulus based on our
personal network of memories and emotions (Bower, 1981).

Through these experiences and the growing networks, we learn to act adaptively in our environment. Our secondary reactions consist of the cognitions, feelings, and behaviors we learned to cope with our experiences. Anxiety occurs in response to a fearful stimulus, either environmental or imaginal. Mowrer's theory suggests that if avoidance is our response we will continue to fear (Mowrer, 1947). In a like manner, if we cognitively avoid (worry) we will continue to feel anxious. Additionally, the frequently catastrophizing thoughts and images of the worry process can increase the fear (incubation) and strengthen the fearful associations in the network.

As the associative network grows larger, the current worry content can be distant from the core fear. As this occurs, it becomes less likely that we will be exposed to the core fear or learn to cope with it. Cognitive avoidance can lead to the maintenance of our fears and anxious reactions.

Frustrative Non-Reward

Frustrative non-reward represents another theoretical avenue by which anxiety, and therefore worry, may develop and maintain. If we expect certain rewards but do not receive them, anxiety can be the consequence. Mineka (1985) concluded that human anxiety could develop through the frustration of important goals. Once we experience this frustration, we may avoid cues associated with this frustration, as suggested by Mowrer.

The frustrative non-reward conceptualization seems particularly relevant and helpful in understanding the development, generalization, and maintenance of worry and anxiety. An aversive conditioning model leading to simple cognitive avoidance seems insufficient, as there are few clear traumatic conditioning events in the history of clients with diffuse anxiety disorders (e.g., agoraphobia or social phobia). Additionally, cognitive avoidance focuses on past negative events whereas the fears of the worrier focus on future events. Frustrative non-reward focuses on the anticipated frustration of not receiving future rewards. This model emphasizes not only past history, but also concerns over potential frustration in the achievement of highly valued, future goals. Particular traumatic conditioning events are unnecessary; instead, we become anxious and worried because we fear that we will not be happy, we will not achieve our goals, we will be failures. We worry because we experience a discrepancy between our envisioned rewards and the perceived reality. Therefore, we learn to fear and avoid not only failure situations, but any goal-oriented activity that may lead to failure and frustration. This encompasses an unlimited number of potential frustration and potential failure scenarios or cues, and is therefore conducive to rapid, broad generalization of anxiety and worry to many cues.

Of course, it is possible to maintain this anxiety through the avoidance of these cues. Additionally, the cues may become so diffuse, broad and numerous that the core fear becomes unclear, less available, and therefore more difficult to access in any effort to change the *status quo*.

Avoidance in this paradigm can halt striving toward goals, or attempts to achieve or succeed. Frustrative non-reward creates an approach-avoidance conflict, a double bind, or "catch-22." If we avoid anxiety by avoiding activity related to the goal, then we may experience depression over a lack of rewards. If we work toward the goal, we may experience the anxiety generated by the fear of not achieving the reward. As Dollard and Miller (1950) suggested, this situation will lead to alternation between approach and avoidance and the resultant emotional states — anxiety and depression. In this way, the model also provides a suggestion as to why anxiety and depression often coincide.

As in an aversive conditioning model, these fears or anxiety can be increased and maintained through the cognitive process of worry. We incubate and increase our fears by periodically imagining and embellishing our goals, then catastrophizing about all the possible, negative repercussions if we fail to achieve them. We maintain our anxiety through cognitively avoiding cues related to the feared outcome.

IMPLICATIONS FOR WOMEN:
EXPLORING THE GENDER DIFFERENCE

Given what we have reviewed about worry, why might women report or experience worry more often than men? As we have already noted, this gender difference may be a reflection of differing sex-role identifications for males and females. Evidence suggests that males and females are perceived differently, treated differently, and reinforced for differing gender-roles from the time of their birth (Kaplan & Bean, 1976). Females are encouraged to be "feminine" and males are encouraged to be "masculine" (Kaplan, 1976). Numerous studies indicate that both genders concur on the characteristics that describe these stereotypic gender-roles and subscribe to them: males report higher levels of masculinity and lower levels of femininity, while females report the converse (cf. Spence & Helmreich, 1978). Broverman, Broverman, Clarkson, Rosenkrantz and Vogel (1970) reported that when asked to describe a person, a male, and a female who were healthy and competent, clinicians of both genders describe the "person" and "male" similarly, but the "female" differently. These descriptions fit the sex-role stereotypes, and describe a healthy female as more "passive" and "dependent."

Therefore, in our society considerable consensus exists regarding the nature of masculine and feminine roles. Worry has been traditionally identified as a feminine, gender-role stereotypic trait by both males and females (Block, 1976). Perhaps as women often endorse a feminine gender-role they are more likely to report worry, a role-congruent trait.

Gender-role research (Bem, 1974; Spence, Helmreich & Stapp, 1975) describes masculine characteristics as more instrumental and agentic and feminine characteristics as more expressive and communal. Worry is an ineffective means of problem-solving and may reflect a feminine, less instrumental style. White (1959) noted that in our traditionally masculine society, women often do not have the opportunity for the experiences that bring about a positive adjustment. Women may worry more because they are unfamiliar or inexperienced with the alternatives. Adopting the feminine role that society reinforces may mean not receiving exposure or training in more effective strategies and coping skills.

We have suggested that worry originates from a basic fear of failure and rejection. These fears are hypothesized as the core of the worry process. Worriers attempt to avoid mistakes, especially those that may generate negative feedback from the social environment. Women may worry more because they experience more situations in which they face potential failure. How might this occur?

Unger (1979) indicated that the most salient role for a female is parental and the most salient role for a male is providing material support for family. Whereas men receive tangible rewards for achievement in their traditional realm, women's role as wife-mother has ambiguous standards for performance, no monetary incentives, and little societal prestige. In light of few rules and overt rewards, women in traditional roles may experience and fear potential failure regardless of their actual performance.

Women in non-traditional or multiple roles may also experience frequent, potential failure situations. The number of women working either through choice or financial necessity continues to increase. However, few role models or other supports exist for professional women (Douvan, 1979). Financial rewards, promotions, and prestige are inequitable in the workplace, and are given to males far more frequently than to females (Gove, 1980; Unger, 1979). Again, women may encounter frustration because they are not allowed to achieve regardless of their abilities or performance.

Additionally, socially acceptable areas of achievement are sex-typed as early as elementary school (Laws, 1978). The qualities associated with wife-mother and career person roles are gender-typed as well and often viewed as incompatible. By traditional definitions these roles are in conflict and not easily merged. Violation of gender-role expectations may result in social disapproval and hostility (Darley, 1979). Here societal norms create a catch-22 with unfortunate and worrisome results. Women will experience and perhaps even accept the socialized view that success in one role means failure in the other.

It has already been noted that traditional spouse and parental roles for women provide them with few tangible rewards. In the workplace, labor is delineated into "male" and "female" jobs. Lloyd and Archer (1981) report that women are overrepresented in low status, low paying jobs regardless of educational level. Because of these continuing inequities, women have less to gain when they do achieve. A female college graduate can expect to be paid at the same level as a male high school drop-out (Laws, 1978). Therefore, it is likely that a woman would experience frustration if she hoped for reasonable rewards such as salary and prestige commensurate with her abilities and education.

A common finding is that women are more likely than men to believe that external forces control their lives. Unger (1979) suggested that this belief is based in fact — females have less power, lower social status, and less economic freedom than their male counterparts (Kaplan & Bean, 1976; Lloyd & Archer, 1981; Maccoby & Jacklin, 1974; Williams, 1979). Because of these differences, Brodsky indicated that although women outnumber men, women are considered a minority " . . . because of stereotyping and discrimination based on their sex that has designated them to inferior status" (1982, p. 138). Women may struggle with the social and economic inequities that exist but over which they have little control. These conflicts and the sense of powerlessness and loss may lead to anxiety and worry through the mechanism of frustrative non-reward.

Thus, fear of failure and rejection, the likely bases of worry, provide a structure for understanding worry in women. The frustrative non-reward paradigm provides an environmental explanation for the more frequent development of anxiety and worry for women in our society.

TREATMENT RESULTS AND IMPLICATIONS

Only a few studies have been conducted on the treatment of worry. Borkovec, Wilkinson, Folensbee and Lerman (1983) suggested that worry could be viewed as an uncontrollable, cognitive habit that occurs in many situations when attention demand is low. Like our habit disorders (smoking, over-eating, psychologically-based insomnias) worry is under poor stimulus control, associated with many environmental stimuli. Outcome studies were begun using an adaptation of Bootzin's stimulus control treatment for insomnia (Bootzin, 1972).

In the first study, subjects in the treatment condition were given the following instructions.

1. Establish a half hour worry period to occur at the same time each day and in the same place.

2. Monitor your worries during the day, learning to quickly identify the beginning of any worry episode.
3. Postpone your worrying as soon as you notice its beginning.
4. Substitute attention to present moment experience or the task at hand.
5. Make use of your worry period to worry intensely about your concerns.

This treatment group was compared with a no treatment control group. A counter-demand statement suggested that subjects would not experience treatment effects until the fourth week. Even with this suggestion, at the end of the third and fourth weeks the stimulus-control group significantly reduced their daily worry. The no treatment control demonstrated no significant change.

The second experiment compared two treatment groups with a no treatment control. Treatment groups were identical except that one had a mental worry period (as in the first study) and the other was instructed to write down their thoughts during the worry period. Again, even with a counter-demand suggestion, treatment groups showed improvement superior to the no treatment group during the third week of application. No differences were found between the mental and written worry period treatments.

In an effort to clarify treatment effects, Folensbee (1984) contrasted two treatments with stimulus control instructions and a placebo condition. The first treatment group received the standard stimulus control training. The second treatment group substituted a problem-solving period for the worry period. The placebo group received simple relaxation training. Folensbee reasoned that without instructions in the application to stress and worry, relaxation would not have therapeutic effects but would be a suitable placebo condition. All subjects were given the counter-demand suggestion.

Ratings of treatment expectancy and credibility were equivalent for all groups, indicating that subjects viewed the placebo condition as a viable treatment. However, as in previous research, both stimulus control groups showed significant improvement over the placebo group. These reductions in worry were noted at the third and fourth weeks of treatment and maintained at a six month follow-up. No differences were found between the two active treatment conditions.

Clearly chronic worriers can learn some control over the worry process. Perhaps worry reduction is due to increased awareness and learning ways to stop the worry process and redirect attention. Perhaps an intensive worry period extinguishes fear responses in some situations.

Symptom reduction is important as the worry process seems to engender general dysphoria, to interfere with attention and performance, and to be an inefficient means of dealing with our life disappointments and frustrations. Perhaps some combination of stimulus controls and skills training in problem-solving, coping relaxation, and assertiveness could enhance the effects reported in experimental treatments.

However, although these approaches clearly have value, they may be insufficient for the depth and complexity of this problem. Worry is likely based on diffuse, social-evaluative fears of failure and rejection. These fears are similar to those found in clients with agoraphobia and generalized anxiety disorder. Theorists have hypothesized an underlying interpersonal basis for these conditions (e.g., Chambless & Goldstein, 1980; Hare & Levis, 1981). Additionally, the threat or fear experienced by worriers is defined in terms of the individual's self-perception and beliefs about how others in society perceive and treat them. Perhaps in merely reducing symptoms we teach clients, and especially women, to simply not worry over real conflicts and inequities. Instead, the clinician may need to go further, exploring the client's definition of goals and values, methods of achieving those goals, and discrepancies between those goals and the supports and strictures imposed by current societal conditions.

Women are socially, politically, and economically disadvantaged. The effects of these circumstances are experienced regardless of whether a woman chooses a traditional or non-traditional gender-role and identification. Women may experience and fear a lack of rewards and potential failures regardless of their abilities and achievements. In treating chronic worry, therapists need to help women increase their self-awareness, and examine their own and societal assumptions about female roles. It is important for clients to be able to cope with frustration and inequity. However, rather than simply increasing comfort and compliance with the restrictive *status quo*, clinicians can assist in the development of clients' independent self-identity and self-determination (Brodsky, 1980).

A final relevant concern is the role that mental health professionals may play in the maintenance of traditional gender-roles and stereotypes (Davidson & Abramowitz, 1980). Gove (1980) suggested that therapists can be agents of personal, political, and social change. The classic Broverman et al. (1970) investigation suggested that clinicians maintained a gender-stereotyped "double standard" for mental health in males and females. Although subsequent analogue and naturalistic research has produced mixed results, the current consensus is that this bias may indeed exist (Davidson & Abramowitz, 1980). It is clear that a therapist's traits, attitudes, and values may have critical effects on clients and their treatment (Abramowitz & Dokecki, 1977; Strupp, 1982). In light of these issues, and to insure ethical treatment, it is crucial that we as therapists examine our own assumptions and prejudices regarding gender-roles and role-congruent behavior.

REFERENCES

Abramowitz, C. V. & Dokecki, P. R. (1977). The politics of clinical judgment: Early empirical returns. *Psychological Bulletin, 84*, 460-476.

Beck, A. T. (1976). *Cognitive therapy and the emotional disorders*. New York: International University Press.

Bem, S. L. (1974). The Measurement of psychological androgyny. *Journal of Consulting and Clinical Psychology, 42*, 155-162.

Block, J. H. (1976). Debatable conclusions about sex differences. *Contemporary Psychology, 21*, 517-522.

Bootzin, R. R. (1972). Stimulus control treatment for insomnia. *Proceedings of the 80th annual convention of the American Pscyhological Association, 7*, 395-396.

Borkovec, T. D. (1979). Pseudo (experiential)-insomnia and idiopathic (objective) insomnia: Theoretical and therapeutic issues. In H. J. Eysenck and S. Rachman (eds.), *Advances in behavior research and therapy* (pp. 27-55). London: Pergamon Press.

Borkovec, T. D., Robinson, E., Pruzinsky, T. & DePree, J. A. (1983a). Preliminary exploration of worry: Some characteristic and processes. *Behavior Research and Therapy, 21*, 9-16.

Borkovec, T. D., Wilkinson, L., Folensbee, R. & Lerman, C. (1983b). Stimulus control applications to the treatment of worry. *Behavior Research and Therapy, 21*, 247-251.

Bower, G. H. (1981). Mood and memory. *American Psychologist, 36*, 129-148.

Brodsky, A. M. (1980). A decade of feminist influence on psychotherapy. *Psychology of Women Quarterly, 4*, 331-343.

Brodsky, A. M. (1982). Sex, race and class issues in psychotherapy research. In J. H. Harvey & M. M. Parks (eds.), *Psychotherapy research and behavior change.* (pp. 123-150). Washington, DC: American Psychological Association.

Broverman, I., Broverman, D., Clarkson, F., Rosenkrantz, P. & Vogel, S. (1970). Sex-role stereotypes and clinical judgment of mental health. *Journal of Consulting and Clinical Psychology, 34*, 1-7.

Chambless, D. & Goldstein, A. (1980). Anxieties: Agoraphobia and hysteria. In A. M. Brodsky & R. Hare-Mustin (eds.), *Women and psychotherapy.* New York: Guilford Press.

Darley, S. A. (1979). Big-time careers for the little woman: A dual-role dilemma. In J. H. Williams (ed.), *Psychology of women: Selected readings.* (pp. 377-387). New York: W. W. Norton & Company.

Davidson, C. V. & Abramowitz, S. I. (1980). Sex bias in clinical judgment: Later empirical returns. *Psychology of Women Quarterly, 4*, 377-395.

Deffenbacher, J. L. (1980). Worry and emotionality. In I. G. Sarason (ed.), *Test anxiety: Theory, research, and applications* (pp. 111-128). Hillsdale, NJ: Lawrence Erlbaum Associates.

Dohrenwend, B. & Dohrenwend, B. (1976). Sex differences and psychiatric disorders. *American Journal of Sociology, 81*, 377-395.

Dollard, J. & Miller, N. E. (1950). *Personality and psychotherapy.* New York: Mc-Graw-Hill.

Douvan, E. (1979). The role of models in women's professional development. In J. H. Williams (ed.), *Psychology of Women: Selected readings.* (pp. 388-400). New York: W. W. Norton & Company.

Dow, M. G. & Craighead, W. E. (1982). Cognition and social inadequacy: Relevance in clinical populations. In P. Trower (ed.), *Cognitive perspectives in social skills training.* Oxford: Pergamon Press.

Eysenck, H. J. (1979). The conditioning model of neurosis. *The Behavioral and Brain Sciences, 2*, 155-199.

Folensbee, R. (1984). *Stimulus control vs. relaxation-placebo in the treatment of chronic worry.* Unpublished doctoral dissertation, The Pennsylvania State University.

Gove, W. R. (1980). Mental illness and psychiatric treatment among women. *Psychology of Women Quarterly, 4*, 345-362.

Green, B. J. (1980). *Depression in early adolescence: An exploratory investigation of its frequency, intensity, and correlates.* Unpublished doctoral dissertation, The Pennsylvania State University, University Park, PA.

Hare, N. & Levis, D. J. (1981). Pervasive ("free-floating") anxiety: A search for a cause and treatment approach. In S. Turner, K. S. Calhoun & H. E. Adams (eds.), *Handbook of clinical behavior therapy.* New York: Wiley & Sons.

Johnson, M. (1980). Mental illness and psychiatric treatment among women: A response. *Psychology of Women Quarterly, 4*, 363-371.

Johnson (1981). Personal Communication.

Kaplan, A. G. (1976). Androgyny as a model of mental health for women: From theory to therapy. In A. G. Kaplan & J. P. Bean (eds.), *Beyond sex-role stereotypes: Readings toward a psychology of androgyny,* (pp. 353-362). Boston: Little, Brown & Company.

Kaplan, A. G. & Bean, J. P. (1976). *Beyond sex-role stereotypes: Readings toward a psychology of androgyny.* Boston: Little, Brown & Co.

Laws, J. L. (1978). Work motivation and work behavior of women: New perspectives. In J. Sherman & F. Denmark (eds.), *Psychology of women: Future directions in research*. New York: Psychological Dimensions.

Liebert, R. M. & Morris, L. W. (1976). Cognitive and emotional components of test anxiety: A distinction and some initial data. *Psychological Reports, 20*, 975-978.

Lloyd, B. B. & Archer, J. (1981). Problems and issues in research on gender differences. *Current Psychological Reviews, 1*, 287-304.

Maccoby, E. E. & Jacklin, C. N. (1974). *The psychology of sex differences*. Stanford: The Stanford University Press.

Mandler, G. & Watson, D. L. (1966). In C. D. Spielberger (ed.), *Anxiety and Behavior*. New York: Academic Press.

McCarthy, P. R. & Borkovec, T. D. (1983, December). *Worry: Basic characteristics and processes*. Paper presented at the Association for the Advancement of Behavior Therapy, Washington, DC.

Metzger, R. L., Miller, M., Sofka, M., Cohen, M., DiMarcno, E., Bigley, T. & Pennock, M. (1983, December). *Information processing and worrying*. Paper presented at the meeting of the Association for the Advancement of Behavior Therapy, Washington, DC.

Mineka, S. (1985). Animal models of anxiety-based disorders. In A. H. Tuma & J. D. Maser (eds.), *Anxiety and the anxiety disorders*. Hillsdale, NJ: Lawrence Erlbaum.

Morris, L. W. & Fulmer, R. S. (1976). Test anxiety (worry and emotionality) changes during academic testing as a function of feedback and test importance. *Journal of Educational Psychology, 68* (10), 817-824.

Mowrer, O. H. (1947). On the dual nature of learning – a re-interpretation of "conditioning" and "problem-solving." *Harvard Educational Review, 17*, 102-148.

Neale, J. M. & Katahn, M. (1968). Anxiety choice and stimulus uncertainty. *Journal of Personality, 36*, 235-245.

Pruzinsky, T. (1983). *An investigation of the personality and cognitive characteristics of worriers and non-worriers*. Unpublished master's thesis, The Pennsylvania State University, University Park, PA.

Sherif, C. W. (1982). Needed concepts in the study of gender identity. *Psychology of Women Quarterly, 6*, 375-398.

Spence, J. T. & Helmreich, R. L. (1978). *Masculinity and femininity: Their psychological dimensions, correlates and antecedents*. Austin, TX: University of Texas Press.

Spence, J. T., Helmreich, R. L. & Stapp, J. (1975). Ratings of self and peers on sex-role attributes and their relation to self-esteem and conceptions of masculinity and femininity. *Journal of Personality and Social Psychology, 32*, 29-39.

Stavosky, J. M. (1986). *An investigation of the relationship of gender and sex-role identity to the self-report of worry and depression*. Unpublished manuscript.

Strupp, H. H. (1982). The outcome problem in psychotherapy: Contemporary perspectives. In J. H. Harvey & M. M. Parks (eds.), *Psychotherapy research and behavior change*. (pp. 39-71). Washington, DC: American Psychological Association.

Unger, R. K. (1979). Toward a redefinition of sex and gender. *American Psychologist, 34*, 1085-1094.

Verbrugge, L. M. (1980). Sex differences in complaints and diagnoses. *Journal of Behavior Medicine, 3*, 327-356.

Veroff, J., Douvan, E. & Kulka, R. A. (1981). *The inner American: A self-portrait from 1957 to 1976*. New York: Basic Books.

Weissman, M. M. (1980). Depression. In A. M. Brodsky & R. Hare-Mustin (eds.), *Women and psychotherapy*. New York: Guilford Press.

White, R. (1959). Motivation reconsidered: The concept of competence. *Psychological Review, 66,* 297-333.

Walowitz, H. M. (1972). Hysterical character and feminine identity. In J. M. Bardwick (ed.), *Readings on the psychology of women.* New York: Harper & Row.

Williams, J. H. (1979). *Psychology of women: Selected readings.* New York: W. W. Norton & Company.

Achievement Related Fears:
Gender Roles and Individual Dynamics

Julia A. Sherman

Fear of failure and fear of success usually hover below awareness, the motives aroused and assuaged without conscious
knowledge. Clients are depressed, anxious, confused, or angry;
they lack confidence, have low self-esteem or marital conflict,
but they rarely say they fear either failure or success. Usually this
needs to be interpreted to them.

Fear of failure means fear of not reaching a particular goal.
Commonly such fear will prevent a woman from even attempting
the goal or she may attempt it but be handicapped by anxiety.
Have you ever walked across a log over a stream? Striding confi-
dently all is well, but if you are afraid that you will fail, suddenly
you do not know where or how to place your feet and clumsiness
and paralysis endanger your very crossing. Such is the effect of
fear of failure.

Though fear of failure exists as a construct in the mind of the
psychologist, in the individual, fear of failure is not easily sepa-
rated from lack of confidence, low self-esteem, low risk taking.
Links between these feelings, sex role and the patient's life situation usually must be made by the therapist since they are not self-
evident to the client.

Julia A. Sherman, PhD, ABPP, is a psychologist in private practice with Madison
Psychiatric Associates, Ltd., 5534 Medical Circle, Madison, WI 53719, and Clinical
Preceptor with the University of Wisconsin, Psychology Department. Her books, artic-
les, and research have dealt with the psychology of women especially in cognitive areas
and psychotherapy. She is author of a forthcoming book, *Woman to Person: Today's
Guide to Mental Health*.

Therapeutic management of fear of failure depends on the individual's capacity for achievement. It is not helpful to encourage a woman to aspire to goals she realistically has little chance to meet. Careful assessment, even psychological testing, may be necessary to know whether a woman rejects a goal because of fear of failure or because she correctly perceives that she cannot achieve it. In some instances she may be considering factors that we don't understand as well as she, such as her disinclination for hard work and study, her emotionality, or poor tolerance for stress. Sometimes our clients know better than we what they can and cannot do.

Fear of failure is usually thought of in the academic or vocational areas, but women fear they cannot conceive a child, deliver it naturally or breast feed it, or they fear they cannot satisfy their husbands, carry off a dinner party, dance, or master tennis. Fear of failure can apply to many goals and these fears are probably more common among women and just as intensely felt as fear of failure in educational or job achievement. Presumably fear of failure research ignores these female role behaviors because they are commonplace; they are not problematic; they do not hinder the onward development of women in the world of intellectual and financial achievement as does math anxiety, for example, which is basically fear of failure in mathematics.

An example of fear of failure was a mildly depressed woman of fifty who wanted a college education but feared she was too old to do the work. I debated whether to give her an ability test since she would be discouraged if it turned out badly, but judging from her conversation, I thought she would do well on the test. Her Full-Scale Wechsler IQ proved to be 140 and I used this as evidence that she could complete college. Without this direct encouragement she might never have attempted college, though she graduated with highest honors.

Men certainly experience fear of failure, but males are consistently more confident than females. The difference is pervasive, except perhaps for some traditional female areas, usually not investigated. In my studies, it was apparent that boys and men are more confident of their mathematical and spatial perception skills, and that their confidence promotes achievement and willingness to set further goals in mathematics (Fennema & Sherman, 1977; Sherman, 1974). Curiously, males overestimate how well they can do while females underestimate how well they can do. Each sex is equally but oppositely inaccurate, but overestimating skill leads to trying new goals while underestimating decreases risk taking. Sex-role linked lack of confidence contributes to women's fear of failure in math, math-related areas and in many other endeavors.

Fear of failure, low confidence and self-esteem are problems not easily dealt with directly in therapy. Lasting change in these areas seems to be a by-product of actions, not goals attained in themselves, thus behavioral methods are a suitable approach. I try to obtain a realistic assessment of the client's ability and recommend that she try out her ability at an appropriate level of difficulty or level of anxiety, if that is the more cogent concept. Some clients will take the chance and others will not; aim low so that the client can experience success. There is no substitute for actually seeing that you can do something. Simple reassurance is hollow.

Another tactic, a more dynamic approach, is to analyze the sources of fear of failure and lack of confidence: women's role, family, ethnic and class expectations, browbeating from others, bad luck, negative experiences. Clients gain encouragement from learning that sources of their fears and low confidence are falsely based.

My client, Sylvia, not her real name of course, combined fear of failure with the impostor syndrome. Sylvia came from a large family of working class people. Her mother had never worked outside of the home; Sylvia was married to an active alcoholic who nonetheless retained a good job, and they had two school-age children. Like the rest of her family, she had no more than a high school education, but she was bright, responsible and hardworking. Before she understood what was happening she was promoted from her clerical job to one of increased pay, responsibility, and considerable power and authority. As an investigator for a state regulatory agency, whole companies were affected by her decisions. To make matters worse, little provision had been made to train her on the job and she had family problems. She was terrified, depressed, had lost weight, and had difficulty sleeping. Everyday she waited for "them" to find her out. Her

job evaluations were positive but this did not assauge her fear
since she had trouble believing them. Resourcefully, she located
a sympathetic co-worker who answered her questions, though
this mentor relationship had to be hidden because the boss expected her to figure it out on her own.

The job and other responsibilities were such a severe strain
(she was skin and bones) that I agreed with her decision to postpone a planned promotion to even more responsible duties. Her
husband wanted her to quit the job entirely, but she liked it; it
was interesting and it paid well. She realized that she would
probably never find as good a job again, given the job market,
her relative lack of education, and there was always the specter in
the back of her mind that her husband's alcoholism might force a
divorce or make a widow of her. She stuck it out. She was placed
on antidepressants and by the end of several sessions she was still
uncomfortable but not panicked. She could place her reaction in
perspective; she had moved off the map of life that her gender
and family background had conferred upon her, but she realized
also that she could move slowly and steadily, finding her way,
mapping new territory. Her family problems, however, continued to be a source of severe strain.

Fear of success (Horner, 1972), that ill-fated concept that
flashed across the skies, has faded as a theoretical construct, but
a true phenomenon of this sort exists. Hyde and Rosenberg
(1976) in their psychology of women textbook say that they
"feel" it exists. I will go further and say that I know it exists, but
let me describe what I mean. Traditional sex roles expected men
to have higher status than women. Because of this, women
brought up in traditional homes never imagined they might have
positions of high status, particularly not public positions of
power. Such possibilities pose conflict for women between desir-
able status and conformity to the traditional female role. These
conflicts may be acutely felt in heterosexual marketability and in
the exquisite wonder and pain of negotiating a love relationship.
Will he love me if he thinks I am smarter than he is? What will he
think if I get a better grade than he does? How will he feel if I
earn more money or if my job is more important? These thoughts
can have "superego" power, "thou shalt not embarrass thy part-
ner's manhood." Violating this dictum can lead to guilt or self-

defeating behavior unless the narrow strictures of traditional feminine sex role expectations are modified. Fear of success is linked to the female sex role and men therefore could not possibly have more of it than women do (Tresemer, 1977), and hoary concepts from psychoanalysis are even more irrelevant (Krueger, 1984).

Fear of a lover's reactions to her success is not merely in the mind of a woman, since there *are* men who resent their partners having more education, money or status. Sometimes it is right up front. "I don't want you to go to work." "I don't want you to go to school." One might suppose that such restrictions would cause open rebellion or divorce, but in my experience women will usually try to make do if the marriage is otherwise adequate and if they can find a way to satisfy their needs. On the other hand, many men are not as distressed about these matters as their partners think they are. It is a delicate job of negotiation to discover what is okay, not okay, and how to change not okay to okay.

The reason I know fear of success exists is because I have experienced it in myself. I was aware of it before Matina Horner publicized it. By high school age I felt that boys might not like me if I were too smart, but I am not aware that this caused me to change my goals at that time. Rather, I quickly decided that I never wanted to marry a man who would be so threatened by my intellect that he would attempt to limit me, nor did I want to marry a man whose nonachievement would create guilt in me for embarrassing his manhood. For this reason, I deliberately read the manuscript of my future husband's first book and made the judgment that I would have psychological room within the relationship for whatever I wanted to do and so it proved to be.

My next salient experience of fear of success was ironic. I was in the kitchen browning meat for a stew and children were playing in the house making quite a ruckus. The telephone rang and the voice on the other end of the line said, "this is Matina Horner." Between the children, the meat sizzling, and the long distance crackle from the east coast to California, it took me a few seconds to process that. After some amenities, Matina got to the point. Would I like to be considered for the position of director of the research institute? Still stirring the meat with one hand and holding the phone with the other hand, I explained that it would not be possible for me to move at that time, thanked her and said goodbye. For the next two days I was haunted by the thought that Matina Horner had not called, but that someone else had called as a joke. Then it dawned on me that I was showing a classic fear of success reaction; I could not believe that Matina Horner was seriously suggesting that I be considered for this position. The phone call was so unexpected and incongruous with my ongoing traditional sex-role behavior that I had difficulty putting it together in a coherent way.

Fear of success and impostor phenomena arise when the individual's script (ego ideal or achievement expectations internalized as a child) do not include success of the type achieved. One of the most common inhibitors of success is the traditional female sex role, but other sources include class or ethnic scripts associated with low achievement and status, and individual scripts in which a parent did not expect achievement from the child. Pauline Clance vividly describes some of these circumstances in her book, *The Imposter Phenomenon* (1985).

Fear of success generates uneasiness, anxiety and guilt. The injunction not to embarrass the manhood of one's mate may extend to any closely associated male. This is a slightly different sex role motive than the one associated with heterosexuality per se. Janet, for example, was extremely bright but her older brother, chosen to be the achiever of the family, was not as bright as she and the achiever role gradually fell upon her by default, but at a psychological cost. As an adult, it affected her relationships with peer males in the working place. She continually found herself protecting them, giving them the advantage and in situations where they might be compared to her, she found that she inevitably sabotaged herself. It was extremely difficult to change her behavior since much of it was at an unconscious level during the crucial moments of interaction. Very focused, hard thinking when these situations arose led to some improvement, but it was an amazingly durable, self-defeating reaction.

Decision making relevant to fear of success begins at least by grade six with the explicit dawning of sexuality (Sherman, 1979, 1983). Girls at that time are even more worried about these issues than later when they are more experienced. Math and science have been seen as the province of males and have thus become affected by sex role expectations. Fortunately in grades six to eight, students typically have little choice in their courses so that girls cannot opt out of math and science courses, but they can study them less, choose less demanding courses, and participate less in extracurricular math and science activities.

A girl's attitude and course are set by a myriad of small decisions and as the years roll by, she is typically less prepared than her male counterpart to deal with math and science. Not all of these influences have to do with fear of success since there are other sex role issues which have even more realistic components. For example, a young woman who places a high value on rearing children may feel that math-related, high level careers are too demanding to combine with being a mother. So far our society has been less than convincing in its efforts to demonstrate otherwise.

Fear of success was amply demonstrated in my interviews with gifted middle school and high school girls (Sherman, 1982, 1983). Their reactions to the question, "Have you ever played dumb?" showed anxiety that their intelligence might harm them in heterosexual relationships. Their stories were often hilarious, but only a minority of them admitted to actually playing dumb themselves. It was the other girls who played dumb (76% and 86%). These young women self-righteously protested how disgusting it was to see the other girls act stupid, suggesting that they may have been protesting too much and that they were unaware of the extent to which they themselves also played dumb.

Despite the influence of the women's movement, I think that fear of success occurs more often than we realize. As a therapist dealing with fear of success, the first task is to identify it, then therapy depends on analysis of sex role issues and encouragement to test assumptions that men will not tolerate success in a woman. Sometimes so many life decisions have been adversely affected by fear of success that it is impossible to repair all of the damage, though improvement is often possible. For example, I have encouraged women with some aptitude in math to take more math, accounting, or computer courses at the technical school level. Their need to support themselves and their children would not permit four year college degrees, but at least movement out of strictly clerical work affords them access to better paying positions.

Amusingly, men also play dumb. Every morning in households all over America one can hear the plaintive cry of the husband, "Where are _____?" You fill in the blank. "Where are the blueberries?" "Where are my gray socks?" "Where is the salt?" "Where are the car keys?" Boys are even taught to play dumb. My grandfather showed my brother how to sew on a button, but I overheard him to say, "You must never let a woman know that you can sew because then she'll expect you to do it."

Playing dumb about women's traditional work helps guarantee that women will maintain responsibility for "their" work. For women, playing dumb may similarly have served to guarantee that men should feel responsible to take care of them financially and in other ways. Sexual division of labor permits more specialization and creates a reciprocity of interdependence between the sexes. Heterosexually oriented persons are often pleased and mildly stimulated by these exchanges even if they have no courtship significance. Currently, however, division of labor is less defined by sex and more defined by opportunity, ability and interest. Though this change was made possible by our more sophisticated society, individuals and families are still reeling from the implications of the new male and female roles and many are living the consequences of these changes without understanding the sources of their confusion, discontent, new opportunities or good fortune.

In summary, fear of failure and fear of success are found in the clinical consulting room but rarely labeled as such by clients. Essential to their management is a behavioral approach and the analysis of sex role effects, along with social class, ethnic, and family influences.

Much of the debunking commentary about fear of failure and fear of success in females has been irrelevant from a feminist perspective. The point is not that men too fear success but that women fear the success of important status for *sex-role reasons*. Likewise, men may well fear failure even more than women, but for *sex-role reasons* males are more self-confident and less often suppose themselves incompetent at the very start.

REFERENCES

Clance, P.R. (1985) *The Impostor Phenomenon*. New York: Bantam.

Fennema, E. and Sherman, J. (1977) Sex-related differences in mathematics achievement, spatial visualization and affective factors. *American Educational Research Journal, 14* 51-71.

Horner, M.S. (1972) Toward an understanding of achievement related conflicts in women. *Journal of Social Issues, 28* 157-175.

Hyde, J.S. and Rosenberg, B.G. (1976), *Half The Human Experience*. Lexington, Massachusetts: Heath.

Krueger, D.W. (1984) *Success and Fear of Success in Women*. New York: Macmillan.

Sherman, J. (1974) Field articulation, sex, spatial visualization, dependency, practice, laterality of the brain and birth order. *Perceptual and Motor Skills, 38,* 1223-1235.

Sherman, J. (1979) Predicting mathematics performance in highschool girls and boys. *Journal of Education Psychology, 71* 242-249.

Sherman, J. (1982) Mathematics the critical filter; a look at some residues. *Psychology of Women Quarterly, 6* 428-444.

Sherman, J. (1983) Girls talk about mathematics and their future: A partial replication. *Psychology of Women Quarterly, 7* 338-342.

Tresemer, D. (1977) *Fear of Success*. New York: Plenum.

*For Product Safety Concerns and Information please contact
our EU representative GPSR@taylorandfrancis.com Taylor & Francis
Verlag GmbH, Kaufingerstraße 24, 80331 München, Germany*

T - #0156 - 270225 - C0 - 229/152/6 - PB - 9780918393418 - Gloss Lamination